W9-BZA-977

1/07

YA
535
KIRK
LAND

OPTICS

SCIENCE & TECHNOLOGY IN FOCUS

OPTICS

Illuminating the
Power of Light

Kyle Kirkland, Ph.D.
and
Sean M. Grady

Facts On File
An imprint of Infobase Publishing

OPTICS: Illuminating the Power of Light

Facts On File, Inc.
An imprint of Infobase Publishing
132 West 31st Street
New York NY 10001

Library of Congress Cataloging-in-Publication Data

Kirkland, Kyle.
Optics : illuminating the power of light / Kyle Kirkland and Sean M. Grady.
p. cm. — (Science and technology in focus)
Includes bibliographical references and index.
ISBN 0-8160-4704-9 (acid-free paper)
1. Optics. 2. Light. 3. Optical instruments. I. Grady, Sean M., 1965– . II. Title.
III. Series: Science & technology in focus.
QC358.K57 2006
535—dc22   2005036736

Facts On File books are available at special discounts when purchased in bulk quantities for businesses, associations, institutions, or sales promotions. Please call our Special Sales Department in New York at
(212) 967-8800 or (800) 322-8755.

You can find Facts On File on the World Wide Web at http://www.factsonfile.com

Text design by Erika K. Arroyo
Cover design by Nora Wertz

Printed in the United States of America

VB Hermitage 10 9 8 7 6 5 4 3 2 1

This book is printed on acid-free paper.

This book is dedicated to my mother, Elizabeth Kirkland,
who is a source of illumination and inspiration
that I can only but faintly imitate.

CONTENTS

ACKNOWLEDGMENTS

Thanks go to the many scientists, physicians, and engineers who provided some of their valuable time and insight, and to Carol L. Sjoberg for acquiring the photographs of the National Ignition Facility. Kyle Kirkland would also like to acknowledge a debt to his former teachers and mentors, who endured an inquisitive and not always obedient pupil, and a bigger debt to Elizabeth Kirkland, who endured a not-so-wonderful son and yet remained a wonderful parent. My appreciation to Frank K. Darmstadt, executive editor, as well as the rest of the staff for their invaluable contributions to the making of this book.

INTRODUCTION

Optics—the science and technology of light—has been a part of civilization for thousands of years. People living in the ancient cities of Egypt and Greece made mirrors of polished metal, and philosophers debated the nature of light and the mechanism of vision. Eyeglasses first appeared in Europe late in the 13th century, and telescopes and microscopes followed, making their first appearance in about 1600.

Optical instruments improved vision and enabled people to see farther and better than ever before. Although scientists have also made considerable progress in understanding what light is and how it works, mysteries remain. Sometimes light appears to be an electromagnetic wave, a propagation of electric and magnetic fields traveling at an astounding 670,320,000 miles per hour (1,080,000,000 km/hr) in space. At other times, light appears to be a stream of tiny particles called *photons*. Waves and particles are quite different—waves are periodic and carry energy in the chain of movement along the wave, while particles are discrete objects that move as a whole. Something can be one or the other but not both; yet light displays the properties of waves and particles, though not at the same time.

Even as some of the secrets of light remain unknown, optical technology continues to advance. Lasers, first developed in 1960, produce a beam of light so narrow and intense that it can cut through metal or travel all the way to the Moon and back, allowing scientists to measure the Earth-Moon distance—248,000 miles (400,000 km)—with an accuracy of a few fingerwidths. Optical fibers are hair-thin strands of glass carrying information in the form of light pulses throughout the world, including much of the data on the Internet. Optical computers may one day use light to solve the trickiest computational problems. *Photonics*—technologies using photons—could be to the 21st century what electronics and electrons were to the 20th.

This book covers the history of optics as both a science and a technology, describing how people struggled toward a better though still incomplete understanding of the nature of light. Vision in life, art, and illusion, the subject of other chapters, proves that while light is a useful phenomenon, people cannot always believe what they see. Later chapters show some of the many ways in which light has been put to work as a tool, including techniques and instruments recently developed or in development that will see the farthest galaxy or detect tiny ripples in space caused by the passage of gravitational waves. From the polished mirror of ancient times to the fiber optics of today, light maintains its power to amaze and illuminate.

THE NATURE OF LIGHT AND VISION

For three separate one-hour periods in July and August of 1971, the astronauts of *Apollo 15* covered their eyes with blindfolds and recorded their observations. This activity was just one of their many duties; the primary goal of *Apollo 15*, crewed by David Scott, James Irwin, and Alfred Worden, was to land on the Moon and return safely to Earth. The mission, like that of the first Moon landing by *Apollo 11* astronauts in July 1969, was successful. Since the *Apollo 15* astronauts had plenty to keep them busy—and plenty to look at—it might seem strange for them to block their vision, even for a few hours. Far more strange is the idea of blindfolded people recording their "observations."

But there was a reason for these experiments, which were also conducted by other Apollo astronauts. Beginning with *Apollo 11*, astronauts reported seeing unexplained flashes of light during the course of their spaceflight. Astronauts commonly described the light as a "spot" or "starlike" flash; *Apollo 15* astronaut David Scott said it resembled a camera's flashbulb seen at a distance. In order to study these lights, astronauts conducted experiments under controlled conditions. For example, the three *Apollo 15* astronauts saw a total of 23 flashes of light in their third hour-long test.

The Saturn V rocket launched the *Apollo 15* astronauts from Kennedy Space Center, Florida, on July 26, 1971. [NASA]

Because of the blindfold, the lights seen by the astronauts could not have been part of the normal vision process. People have long known the eye is responsible for vision, since an injured eye results in a loss of vision. What people did not so easily appreciate is the nature of light—and the role light plays in the process of vision.

Why People Can See

Vision is the most important sense in humans. Much of the complex activity of the human brain occurs in the region known as the cerebral cortex, a layered sheet of *cells* covering the outer surface of the brain's *cerebral hemispheres.* More than half of the cerebral cortex in humans contributes in part to vision. For example, an area called the primary visual cortex—located in the occipital lobe, at the back of the brain—identifies line segments and other basic components of a visual scene: light and shade, different colors, the outline of objects, and so on.

Other areas of the cerebral cortex receive this information and process it further, enabling objects to be identified and perceived.

But it all starts with the *retina*, located at the back of the eye. In a process discussed later in this book, the cells of the retina convert light into electrical and chemical signals. The first step happens when light enters the pupil of the eye and strikes the retina. The pupil looks black because it is a hole into the eye, and the eye absorbs most of the light so that little escapes. The process of seeing begins with this absorption of light; if the eye failed to absorb light, it would be poorly suited for its job. This caused some confusion among ancient scientists, such as the Greek philosophers Pythagoras and Plato, who believed that the eye worked by emitting rays instead of receiving them. Under this mistaken notion, vision occurred when the eye probed its surroundings by bouncing rays off the objects to be seen.

This is not a completely far-fetched idea—the same principle underlies *sonar* (sound navigation and ranging), where sensitive instruments map their surroundings by emitting high-frequency sound

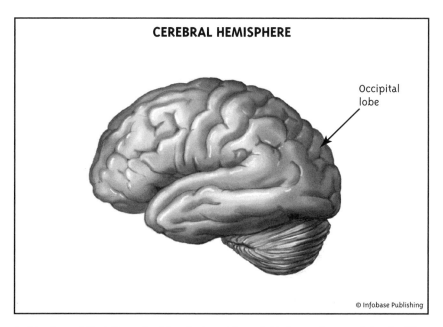

CEREBRAL HEMISPHERE

Occipital lobe

© Infobase Publishing

A side view of the left cerebral hemisphere. The wrinkled covering consists of a thin, layered network of brain cells called the cerebral cortex.

waves and detecting the echoes. Animals such as bats and dolphins also use sonar. Their squeaks are too high-pitched for humans to hear but allow the animals to locate prey or obstacles in the dark and, in the case of dolphins, murky water.

Vision works differently. All things capable of being seen must either emit light—like a lamp or the Sun—or reflect light that has been emitted by some other source, as is the case with the pages of this book. Light striking an object can be either reflected or absorbed, and all objects reflect some portion of the light and absorb the rest. Part of the reflected light enters the eye of a viewer and is seen; an object that absorbs all light striking it and reflects none would be invisible. (The only known object capable of this is a black hole. These massive, dense bodies in space have such strong gravity that nothing, not even light, can escape—so all the light falling on a black hole is absorbed.)

A blindfolded person cannot see because light cannot enter the eye. But if so, what were the Apollo astronauts seeing when they performed their experiment?

One possibility is that the astronauts were not seeing light at all. The structure of the brain is a little like a set of labeled telephone lines: A pathway called the *optic nerve* carries information from the eye to the brain, and brain cells receiving these signals automatically interpret them as visual. This is like receiving a telephone call from a number with an area code of 215. Although the receiver may not recognize the rest of the number, the call must have originated in Philadelphia, Pennsylvania, since 215 is an area code for telephone numbers in this city. The brain assumes signals coming from the eye are visual—a reasonable assumption—and any stimulation of a person's retina or optic nerve will cause the person to "see" light, no matter how the stimulation occurred. People who experience a jarring knock to the head may see "stars" because the force of the blow stimulated their visual system.

The light flashes seen by the astronauts may have been caused by cosmic rays. Cosmic rays consist of tiny particles, such as positively charged atomic particles called protons, that travel through space at extremely high speed. Outside of a planet's atmosphere, space is mostly empty—a vacuum—but there are a few atoms or parts of atoms, along with a small amount of dust, floating around. A few of these particles, such as cosmic rays, move at enormous speeds and are tiny and fast enough to zip right through many materials, including the skin of a space craft and eye shades. The hypothesis is that the cosmic-ray particles entered the eyes and somehow stimulated the retinas of the astronauts, who then saw flashes of light.

But there is another possibility. Perhaps something, such as these cosmic rays, got into the eye and somehow emitted light that the retina detected. This explanation of course relies on some means of producing light. But the generation of light is not difficult: Light is electromagnetic radiation, which comes in quite a few different varieties.

The Electromagnetic Spectrum

Although it is not obvious, light is related to electric and magnetic forces. Light behaves in many cases like an electromagnetic wave, propagating through empty space or a *transparent* piece of matter. Physicists describe electric and magnetic forces as creating a *field*—a region in space that exerts electrical or magnetic forces. Electricity and magnetism are interrelated: A changing electric field produces a magnetic field, and a changing magnetic field produces an electric field. For example, a flow of electric charges such as an alternating current (AC) through a wire or a coil generates a varying magnetic field, which in turn generates an electric field in another, nearby coil and causes a current to flow in this coil. This is how transformers carry electricity into homes; a large quantity of AC from the power company induces a small amount of AC across the coils, so that a house receives electricity but does not require a direct (and dangerous) connection to the power company.

Electromagnetic radiation such as light consists of electric and magnetic fields interacting in a similar way. The electric field varies in time and generates a time-varying magnetic field; the magnetic field generates an electric field, and so on. The electromagnetic disturbance propagates like a wave, with electric and magnetic fields alternatively generating each other, and people often represent light as a wave, as shown in the figure. Like all events that repeat over time, waves have a *frequency*—the number of cycles that occur per second, usually given in units of *Hertz* (cycles per second)—and a *wavelength*, the length of one full cycle. Light travels through space remarkably fast, with a speed of 186,200 miles per second (300,000 km/s)—670,320,000 miles per hour (1,080,000,000 km/hr).

The properties of electromagnetic radiation depend on the frequency and wavelength. Waves with high frequencies have a lot of energy and are often dangerous, while low-frequency waves are less

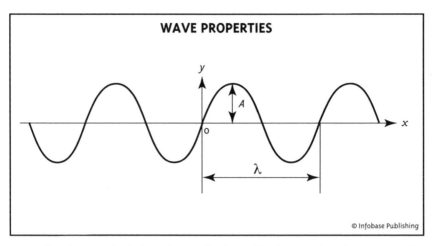

Properties of a wave include *A*, the amplitude, and λ, the wavelength. Frequency is the number of cycles (full wavelengths) that occur per second.

energetic. The frequency is related to the wavelength in a straightforward manner: A high-frequency wave has a short wavelength, and a low-frequency wave has a long wavelength.

Frequency and wavelength are so important that physicists use them to classify the *spectrum* of electromagnetic radiation. High frequencies, such as *X-rays* and *gamma rays*, form one end of the electromagnetic spectrum, and low frequencies, such as *radio waves*, form the other end. Gamma rays can have a frequency of 10^{20} Hertz or higher, while the radio waves that carry music and news have a frequency trillions of times lower—about 1 million Hertz, for example (a typical AM radio station). Visible light comes somewhere in the middle, in the range of 425–750 trillion Hertz—human eyes can detect only this narrow band of frequencies. Most of this book deals with visible light because of its importance in human vision and, of course, optics.

Illumination from the Atomic Realm

One model, or representation, of light is the propagation of electromagnetic waves, as discussed above. (Later chapters in this book describe another and equally valid model of light—a particle called a *photon*.) But what gets the waves started in the first place?

The basic sources for light and the rest of the electromagnetic spectrum are electric charges in motion. Often this involves the tiny negatively charged particles in atoms called *electrons*. Electrons orbit the positively charged nucleus of an atom, but the orbits vary—some have more energy than others. Electrons can change their orbits and often do, making transitions from orbits with one energy level to ones with a different energy level. When electrons jump from a high-energy orbit to a lower one, electromagnetic radiation carries off the difference in energy. When this involves a small amount of energy, the emission of radiation consists of radio waves or other low-frequency waves. Higher amounts of energy create light. In the opposite process, an electron jumping from a low-energy orbit to a higher one absorbs electromagnetic energy; the energy pushes the electron into the high-energy orbit.

Another method of light generation involves the movement of a charged particle at extremely high speeds—for instance, the speed of cosmic rays. This is the process that may play a role in the light flashes seen by astronauts.

According to modern physics theory, the speed of light in a vacuum is the fastest possible speed for any object in the universe. But this does not mean that nothing can move faster than light; it simply means that nothing can move faster than 186,200 miles per second (300,000 km/s). Light slows down when it travels through matter, such as glass or water. The human eye is filled with a fluid that slows light by about 25 percent, and there is nothing to stop a tiny, amazingly fast particle from exceeding this speed in the fluid. Although the particle will eventually bump and grind its way to a stop, its initial speed can be faster than light in this particular substance. When electrically charged particles such as cosmic rays travel through a material at a speed exceeding the speed of light in that material, they emit electromagnetic radiation, called Cherenkov radiation (after the Russian physicist Pavel Alekseyevich Cherenkov, who won the 1958 Nobel Prize in physics for explaining this effect).

Therefore, another explanation of the light flashes seen by astronauts is that cosmic rays may be emitting Cherenkov radiation while inside the eye. The retina absorbs this light, and the astronauts see a flash, even if they happen to be blindfolded at the time. The same process would also happen to people on the surface of Earth, except that the cosmic rays are slowed down by traveling through miles of atmosphere and most of them are moving too slowly when and if they finally reach the ground.

No one is sure what causes the light flashes seen in space. Perhaps there are many causes; both retinal stimulation and Cherenkov radiation might be occurring, and maybe other processes that scientists have yet to find.

This is true of many aspects of light and its properties: People have discovered a great deal about the nature of light and vision, but the subject is complicated enough to defy a complete understanding. Since the story of the development of optics coincides with the investigation of light, the next few chapters describe some of the important mysteries that scientists solved while studying light and the early optical devices.

2

GLIMMERS OF UNDERSTANDING

By 212 B.C.E., the battle for Syracuse had raged for several years. The powerful Roman legions besieged the Greek seaport colony, located on the island of Sicily in the Mediterranean Sea. The Greek warriors held firm, bolstered by one of the most famous scientists of the ancient world, Archimedes, until at last the exhausted city fell to the onslaught of the troops of General Marcus Claudius Marcellus. In 212 B.C.E., the Romans captured Syracuse and killed the great Archimedes.

According to accounts of the siege, Archimedes had spent much of his last few years developing ingenious weapons to defend his city. These weapons included levers and catapults by which the Greek defenders hurled heavy stones and debris at the invaders. Ancient writers also mentioned another, unspecified weapon, used by Archimedes to hurl fire, and a legend grew out of this. The brilliant scientist and engineer, it was said, made giant bronze mirrors that reflected and focused the Sun's rays on Roman ships, setting them on fire.

Archimedes was certainly ahead of his time in many ways, including optics. Whether Archimedes really constructed and used mirrors in the siege of Syracuse is not known, but he and other scientists achieved the beginning of an understanding of light and its applications.

Exploring Light in Ancient Civilizations

Another notable Greek scientist and mathematician, Euclid, lived about the same time as Archimedes and is chiefly noted today for his work on geometry. But Euclid also studied optics. To his mind—influenced, perhaps, by the beauty and simplicity of geometry—light traveled in straight lines, and Euclid used diagrams consisting of rays to show the paths. Reflection occurs when a light ray strikes a surface at some angle and then bounces off. The reflected ray makes the same angle relative to the *normal*—an imaginary line perpendicular to the surface—as the original ray.

Ptolemy is yet another Greek scientist who studied optics but who is more famous for other work. Thriving about 300 years after Archimedes, Ptolemy—like most of the gifted ancient thinkers—did not limit himself to a single subject, and he is best known today for his astronomical studies. For many centuries, people accepted Ptolemy's heliocentric model of the solar system, in which the Sun and planets revolve around Earth. This model is wrong, of course, as was shown in the 16th century by the Polish astronomer Nicolas Copernicus (1473–1543), but Ptolemy's ingenuity remains admirable. In his optical research, Ptolemy noticed that light seems to *refract*—bend—as it travels through materials, including Earth's atmosphere. Atmospheric refraction is important in astronomy for many reasons and affects the apparent position of the stars—though it was not until the time of Danish astronomer Tycho Brahe (1546–1601) that astronomers corrected their star charts for this effect.

Many observers noticed, even before Ptolemy, that light seems to bend. A partially submerged stick seems to bend at the place where it enters the water. A coin, placed in the bottom of an empty metal cup, seems to move when the cup fills with water. Although light generally travels in straight lines, sometimes it does not, and people realized that the bending of light allows it to be focused, or concentrated. The Greek dramatist Aristophanes, who lived several centuries before Archimedes, wrote about a glass for burning parchment and wax tablets. Archaeologists have discovered small crystal *lenses* made thousands of years ago (though their exact purpose is unknown).

The effect of the "burning mirrors" supposedly made by Archimedes was due to reflection, not refraction, but the end result on the Roman ships would have been the same. The warmth of sunlight falling on exposed skin is comfortable; yet when concentrated on a small area—focused by either bending or reflecting the rays—light can start fires. While it seems possible that a clever man such as Archimedes may have been able to design such a device, several modern researchers doubt this happened. In the 1992 paper "Reflections of the 'Burning Mirrors of Archimedes," published in the *European Journal of Physics*, A. A. Mills and R. Clift of Leicester University in the United Kingdom concluded that the light would not have been powerful enough to set wooden ships on fire. The Discovery Channel program *Mythbusters* demonstrated the same thing: In an episode aired in 2004, experimental attempts failed to ignite ships under realistic conditions. Doubters have also questioned why the feat of the burning mirrors did not ever seem to be duplicated in history; if it had been successful, armies would have been likely to try it again and again.

Optics in the Middle Ages and the Renaissance

The burning mirrors of Archimedes may be a myth, but reflection and refraction made their mark on the world. Despite the slow progress during the Middle Ages, toward the end of that period, the science of optics blossomed and bore a particularly important "fruit"—an application of optics whose prevalence and importance has not diminished over the course of 700 years.

The Middle Ages, beginning around the time Rome fell to the Visigoths in 410 and lasting almost a thousand years, was a time of hardship in Europe. Unstable or restrictive political and economic systems did not encourage science, and the gifted thinkers of those days spent their time studying philosophical or religious matters. Scientific research continued but not by Europeans. The best scholars belonged, to the Arabs who lived in northern Africa, the Middle East, and parts of southern Europe.

The most accomplished Arab who studied optics during this time was Abu Ali al-Hasan Ibn al-Haytham (965–1040), known today as Alhazen. Alhazen spent most of his time in Egypt and wrote seven books on optics that were later translated and read by European scientists. With flawless logic and a profound understanding of the scientific method, Alhazen was responsible for many advances in optical science.

Among the subjects tackled by Alhazen was vision. As discussed in chapter 1, most of the earlier scientists believed that eyesight depended on rays emitted by the eye—according to this theory, people see because rays shoot out of the eye and bounce off objects, reflecting back to the eye. Alhazen argued there is no need for the eye emissions because only the reflected light is necessary for vision. Rays from any source will suffice, and they need not come from the eye. Teaching that vision occurs because of sunlight reflecting from visible objects, Alhazen formulated the modern theory of vision.

Alhazen also studied the focusing of light. For instance, the burning mirror of Archimedes—had he built it—would have needed a particular shape, called *paraboloid*. A parabola, such as the graph of the function x^2, revolved around the axis produces a paraboloid. A paraboloid mirror focuses light to a point, whereas a mirror whose reflective surface has a spherical shape does not precisely focus the light. Although the ancient Greeks had a notion this was true, they were fond of the spherical shape because of its symmetry and were reluctant to find fault with it. Alhazen decisively proved the properties of paraboloid and spherical mirrors.

The laws of optics, to be discussed later in this book, were essential in developing the subject to its fullest extent; yet clever experimenters discovered some optical applications by trial and error. Ptolemy mentioned magnification of lenses, and the Roman emperor Nero watched the Coliseum games with an emerald held up to his eye (though he probably used the jewel because it shaded his view with a green color, not for any purpose of magnification). The possibility of using focused light to improve vision would seem to have occurred to people quite early on, but eyeglasses—one of the most enduring legacies of optics—did not appear until near the end of the Middle Ages and the beginning of the Renaissance.

Europe emerged from the Middle Ages with a fresh outlook. It was a time of great change, some good and some bad. The bubonic plague, or Black Death, raged through the Continent in the 14th century with frightening devastation, killing a third or more of the people. But improvements came as well, and the rigid economic and political constraints melted away. Science and technology again flourished in the more open, advanced societies.

In 1268, English philosopher Roger Bacon (1214–92) discussed the benefits of using a *convex lens* while reading. A convex lens is a glass that is thicker in the middle than at the edges, and Bacon noted that if the lens was held at an appropriate distance, the letters on the page increased in size. Twenty years later, an Italian manuscript also mentions spectacles to improve vision. At some point during this period, the development of eyeglasses occurred, though historians have been unable to specify exactly when it happened or the identity of the original inventor. The first known picture of eyeglasses is seen in a painting by Tommaso da Modena in 1352: A man is wearing what any person today would easily recognize as eyeglasses. More than a thousand years had passed since Ptolemy, but the craft of making lenses without unacceptable blurring was not easy to develop—particularly in the Middle Ages when there was so little freedom to explore and discover new things.

Sir Isaac Newton's "Opticks"

The spirit of exploration and discovery soared during the Renaissance and for a long time afterward, continuing to the present day. One of the greatest achievers of all time was Sir Isaac Newton (1642–1727).

Newton published his optical work in the book *Opticks* in 1704. Unlike many of the scholarly books of the time, Newton wrote *Opticks* in English instead of Latin, and it became his most widely read scientific volume. (Newton wrote an earlier book in Latin on motion and gravitation—*Philosophiae Naturalis Principia Mathematica* [*Mathematical Principles of Natural Philosophy*]—that was later translated into English.) In *Opticks*, Newton recorded his experiments with light and the conclusions he drew from them. One of his most important conclusions came from a simple set of experiments involving nothing but a pair of prisms.

A prism is a triangular-shaped piece of glass. Long before Newton's time, people knew that the white light from the Sun passing through a prism separated into all the colors of the rainbow, but they believed the prism was doing something to color sunlight. Newton showed this was not true with two experiments. First he singled out one of the colored lights—green, for instance—and let it pass through another prism. Only green light emerged, suggesting that prisms were not changing light. In another experiment, Newton let the separated colors of one prism pass through another prism; the second prism undid the separation of the first, producing white light. From these experiments,

Sir Isaac Newton [1642–1727]—Biography

Born in Woolsthorpe, England, on Christmas day in 1642—the same year that another famous scientist, Galileo Galilei, died—Newton was a sickly and underweight infant who was not expected to live. Yet he grew strong and became one of the top pupils in his school. At the tender age of 19, Newton went to Cambridge University in Cambridge, England, where he encountered courses based mostly on the ancient Greek philosophers—not at all to his liking. Newton preferred to use his own reasoning skills and to explore the world of nature by doing experiments. In 1665, when the college closed for a while because of an epidemic, Newton continued his studies at home. During this time, he laid the groundwork for much of his thinking on calculus, gravitation, motion, and optics.

Newton finished his degree and stayed at Cambridge for three decades, becoming a mathematics professor in 1669. He was reluctant at first to publish many of his discoveries, apparently because he was sensitive to criticism—which in science both then and now is a large part of the process of deciding what is correct and what is not. Since Newton's work was original and groundbreaking, he could be expected to receive even more critical examination from skeptical scientists. Newton eventually overcame his shyness and published his results; he was a careful scientist, and his work withstood criticism and the test of time.

Newton's interests ranged widely and included gravitation (he discovered the universal law of gravitation), motion (he formulated

Newton correctly reasoned that white light is actually a mixture of colored light.

Newton examined many other aspects of light, stating his ideas in the form of "queries" at the end of *Opticks*. One of the most profound questions about light is its nature—whether it is a wave or a particle or something else. Earlier scientists such as the Greeks and Arabs had not attacked this issue with much vigor, being satisfied more with studying what light does than what it is. Newton stated that he was unsure of the answer, but he leaned toward the belief that light consisted of a stream of particles since light seems to travel in straight lines—and perhaps because Newton was familiar with particles in his studies of three of the most important laws of motion, known today as Newton's laws), mathematics (he developed the techniques known as calculus, needed to solve important problems in physics), and optics. Newton's scientific advances were so enormous that many people today regard him as the greatest scientist who ever lived. His contemporaries had no less respect, and in 1705, Newton became Sir Isaac when he was the first person in the United Kingdom to be knighted for scientific achievement.

Lacking any sense of humor—few people ever saw him smile or laugh—Newton was a stern man who never married. After he became famous as a scientist, he elected to take a job that would earn him considerable money, and

Sir Isaac Newton made significant contributions to mathematics, physics, astronomy, and optics. [AIP Emilio Segrè Visual Archives]

so in 1696, he accepted a position at the Royal Mint. He became Master of the Mint three years later. Newton died on March 20, 1727, and England mourned the loss of its most prestigious scientist, burying him in an elaborate ceremony at Westminster Abbey.

motion and gravitation. Such was Newton's reputation that despite his lack of confidence, many subsequent scientists, showing a lapse in critical judgment, assumed without question that Newton was right. As described in the following chapter, this heralded one of the greatest scientific showdowns—with a strange, unpredictable ending.

FOLLOWING THE LIGHT

Philosophers in the ancient times believed that light was instantaneous—it traveled at infinite speed. This must be so, they reasoned, since they could see the distant Moon and stars immediately after opening their eyes. With eyelids firmly shut, they lifted their faces to the night sky and then opened their eyes; the starry points of light appeared at once.

Although these early scientists based their belief on an experiment, they misinterpreted the results because of an incorrect assumption—they thought the eye emits rays in the process of seeing. If this were true, then the rays must have infinite speed to travel from the eye to the heavenly bodies and back in so short a time. But as discussed in the previous chapter, the Arab scholar Alhazen showed that the eye sees by the light emitted or reflected from visible bodies, and so the ancient experiment proves nothing about the speed of light—the light to see with is always there, whether the eyes are open or not.

Light became better understood in the Renaissance, but questions about its nature and speed remained. If light consisted of a stream of particles, as Sir Isaac Newton suggested, then these particles would not likely travel at "infinite" speed. A wave would take time to propagate as well. The true nature of light proved to be surprising, and astonished scientists discovered that light is merely one small part of a much broader and mostly invisible electromagnetic spectrum.

Waves and Interference

Scientists of the late 18th and early 19th centuries did not at first suspect any involvement of electricity and magnetism in the propagation of light. Many scientists during this period accepted Newton's hypothesis that light was a stream of particles, made up of some incredible small and wispy material.

One scientist who decided to test this hypothesis rather than accept it uncritically was British physician and physicist Thomas Young (1773–1829). Young had many scientific, medical, and philosophical interests, but one of his most famous experiments involved optics. In about 1800, Young performed what is now known as the double-slit experiment. The result was surprising: Light is a wave. Although Young's interpretation of his experiment was not accepted at first, he

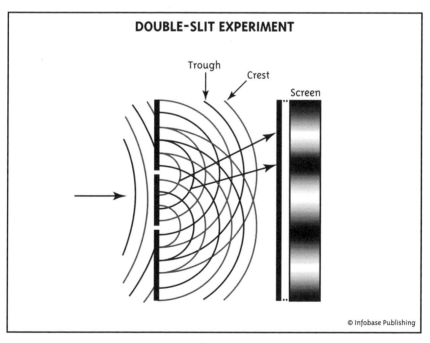

DOUBLE-SLIT EXPERIMENT

© Infobase Publishing

The light waves pass through the two slits from the left, then travel various distances to the screen. Waves from the two slits overlap and interfere, producing light and dark bands.

Thomas Young (1773–1829)—Biography

Thomas Young was a polymath—a rare word these days, describing an equally rare characteristic. A polymath knows a great deal about a number of different subjects. In today's world, people tend to specialize, focusing their time and attention on only one subject; there are people who study the physics of materials, or speak many different languages, or treat eye diseases, but no one does all three. Young was just such a person, and his knowledge encompassed the whole world; if he had lived in modern times, he could have undoubtedly won fame and wealth as a contestant on a television game show like *Jeopardy!*

Young was born in Milverton, England, on June 13, 1773, the 10th child of his family. His intellectual talent began early: By age two, he had mastered reading, and as a teenager, he was fluent in more than 10 languages, including Greek and Latin. He studied medicine at London and Edinburgh in the United Kingdom and Göttingen in Germany. In 1797, he turned his attention to science at Emmanuel College in Cambridge, England, and in that year, a relative died and left him a considerable fortune. This money freed Young from the necessity of earning a living and let him pursue his studies, although he continued to practice medicine. He was elected a fellow of the Royal Society—an old and prestigious

eventually won over the scientific community and became one of the most pivotal figures in the history of optics.

Today scientists often reproduce Young's experiment with a double-slit apparatus shown in the figure on page 17. Light from a bright source travels through two small slits in a wall and falls on a blank screen. (In Young's original experiment, he split a narrow beam of light with a thin piece of cardboard, but the effect was the same: The two beams hit a screen.) A stream of particles confined in this way would make two bright spots on the screen, one for each beam. What Young observed was much different—the screen showed a series of bright and dark bands.

Young correctly reasoned that the bands were due to *interference*. Two or more waves will interfere with one another if they occupy the same space at the same time, just as the ripples from stones tossed in a pond make interesting patterns on the surface of the water. The figure on page 20 shows an example of interference. Waves have crests (peaks) and troughs (valleys). When two or more waves overlap, the resulting

British organization devoted to science—and served as its foreign secretary, in which capacity Young's skill in languages was useful.

His scientific achievements were broad. In addition to optics, Young studied elasticity—the property of materials to regain their shape when compressed or dented—and scientists acknowledged his work by naming a measure of elasticity Young's modulus in his honor. His work on vision explained how the eye adjusts its focus by changing the curvature of the lens, and he described astigmatism, the disorder resulting in blurry vision. He made advances in the study of the heart

Thomas Young showed that light was a wave [AIP Emilio Segrè Visual Archives]

and circulatory system, and his theory of color vision, based on three primary substances, continues to be accepted today.

Young died on May 10, 1829, in London.

motion is a summation of the individual waves—one wave interferes with the motion of another, and the result is sometimes much different than either of the component waves. When one wave's crest aligns with the trough of another, equal-sized wave, the waves cancel, and there is no motion. When crests align, the resultant wave is big.

In the double-slit experiment, the two beams overlap on the screen, and interference causes the bands, called *interference fringes*. The two beams travel a different distance to most parts of the screen because they take a different path—one slit is closer than the other, except for the center or middle of the screen, which lies midway between the slits. Because the distance is different, the light waves from the two beams hit the screen at a different *phase* in their cycle: One wave may be a crest, but the other wave, traveling a slightly longer distance, may be in a trough. At one point on the screen, both waves might be at a crest, in which case the screen is bright, and at another point, a short distance away, a crest and trough align and cancel to create a dark band.

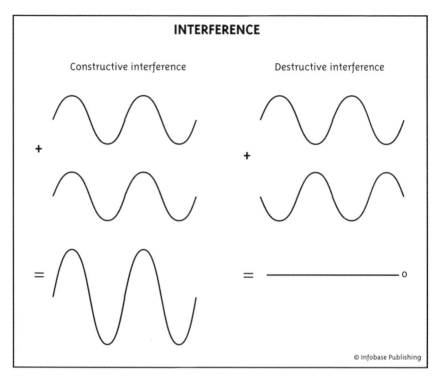

When the combining waves are in phase—the crests and troughs align—then constructive interference occurs. In destructive interference, the waves are out of phase and cancel. Combinations of waves that are partially in phase give results between these two extremes.

The alternating light and dark bands stretch across the screen. Since particles do not cancel one another, this experiment shows that light must be a wave.

Electricity, Magnetism, and Electromagnetic Waves

After Young showed that light was a wave, people wondered what kind of wave it was. Scottish mathematician and physicist James Clerk Maxwell (1831–79) found the answer. Maxwell discovered that light is an electromagnetic wave.

James Clerk Maxwell (1831–1879)—Biography

Few people would expect a person with the childhood nickname of "Dafty" to go on to make great achievements in science and mathematics. Yet Maxwell, who was often absorbed in his own thoughts as a boy, showed promise early in his career. Born on June 13, 1831, at Edinburgh, Scotland, Maxwell enrolled in Edinburgh University at age 16, and in two years, while still a student, he contributed several papers to the Royal Society of Edinburgh. Later, Maxwell attended Trinity College in England. He impressed his mathematics professors at Trinity and graduated in 1854 with the second-highest score in the mathematics exam. In 1856, Maxwell obtained a position at Marischal College, Aberdeen, as a professor of physics.

James Clerk Maxwell discovered the equations that govern electromagnetic interactions. [AIP Emilio Segrè Visual Archives]

Like Thomas Young, Maxwell's knowledge and interests ranged widely. His study of color led him to discover that full-color photographs could be taken by the combination of only three different colors—red, green, and blue. He made an important contribution to astronomy when he studied Saturn's rings and concluded they could not be stable over time if they were solid or fluid; instead, Maxwell proposed that the rings consist of many scattered particles, revolving around the giant planet in confined orbits. He also formulated statistical equations describing the velocities of atoms and molecules in a gas, and related this motion to the temperature of gases. This work was instrumental in the development of the physics of thermodynamics (the study of heat and other forms of energy).

In 1864, Maxwell presented to the Royal Society a set of four mathematical equations that describes all the behavior of electric and magnetic fields. Physicists are always looking for methods to simplify their findings and to present theories in a beautifully clear, concise manner—

(continues)

(continued)
the simpler the better. Although Maxwell's equations are complex (and will not be discussed here), they are powerful in that they capture the entire essence of a complicated phenomenon—electromagnetism—with a minimum of equations. Many scientists regard Maxwell's achievement as one of the most significant contributions to theoretical physics of all time. Maxwell did for electromagnetism what Newton did for gravitation and motion.

In 1871, Maxwell became a professor of physics at Cambridge University (Newton's old school) and remained there until he died from cancer on November 5, 1879.

It is not obvious that light has anything to do with either electricity or magnetism. Electricity and magnetism would not seem to be obviously related either, but research carried out by Danish physicist Hans Christian Oersted (1777–1851) showed that electric currents have magnetic fields, and British physicist Michael Faraday (1791–1867) demonstrated how changing electric and magnetic fields can induce one another. Maxwell admired Faraday and tried to fit Faraday's experimental results into a mathematical and theoretical framework. His brilliant success assured Maxwell of a place in the scientific hall of fame.

While formulating a set of equations describing electromagnetism, Maxwell noticed that the formulas predicted the existence of electromagnetic waves propagating in space. A changing electric field generates a changing magnetic field, which in turn generates an electric field, and so on. According to the equations, these waves travel through space at a velocity of roughly 186,200 miles per second (300,000 km/s). This velocity is the same as light. Maxwell decided this was no coincidence and drew an astonishing conclusion: Light is a propagating electromagnetic wave.

Maxwell's theory was not proof. But the proof followed soon after, when the German physicist Heinrich Hertz (1857–94) produced a type of electromagnetic wave called a radio wave in 1886. Hertz's transmission was weak, and only a few yards of distance separated his transmitter—basically a spark discharge—and receiver, which was only a hoop of wire. But the velocity, reflection, and refraction were the same as light, so Hertz proved that electromagnetic waves exist and behave exactly the same as light.

Measuring the Speed of Light

Maxwell needed to know the speed of light in order to make comparisons with his theory, but he did not have to go out and measure it himself; this had already been done. In 1849, the French physicist Armand Fizeau (1819–96) calculated the speed of light from his experiment involving a rotating, toothed wheel. Fizeau shined pulses of light through the gaps in the wheel and observed the light after it had bounced off a mirror some distance away and returned through the wheel. But when the wheel turned at a certain speed, the teeth blocked the reflection, which Fizeau noted; the pulse entered the gap and reflected from the mirror, but in the time required for the light to make it back to the wheel, the wheel had rotated, and the gap was no longer there. By a careful determination of the wheel's speed and the distance to the mirror, Fizeau calculated the speed of light.

This process was later refined by American physicist Albert Michelson (1852–1931), who took into account factors such as refraction. Michelson also developed other methods to measure the speed of light, and his accuracy won the praise of his colleagues. But Michelson is best known for pioneering an instrument called an *interferometer* and using it in an experiment involving the speed of light that gave a most perplexing result. In recognition of Michelson's contribution to optics, he received the 1907 Nobel Prize in physics, the first American to do so. (The Nobel Prizes began in 1901, and only a living person may receive one—the purpose of the prizes is to stimulate current research—so many deserving scientists of the past, such as Newton, Young, and Maxwell, missed out.)

The basis for the interferometer is the interference of waves. As in Young's double-slit experiment, the summation of waves having different phases produces interference fringes. In Young's experiment, the fringes occur because of the different pathways taken by the two beams of light. In Michelson's interferometer, the fringes would occur if two beams of light traveled at different speeds. But Michelson and his collaborator, Edward Morley (1838–1923), did not see any fringes. This was the perplexing result.

When Maxwell and Hertz showed that light is an electromagnetic wave, people began to wonder what the waves move through. Since waves are a motion in some sort of medium—jump ropes, guitar strings, water, among others—physicists wanted to learn about the medium for

Albert Michelson (1852–1931)—Biography

Today most notable university professors obtain their position through a lengthy process that involves an advanced degree, such as the Ph.D. But in Michelson's time, many professors earned their positions by various means, and the journey Michelson took included a long tour of duty with the navy.

Michelson was born in Strelno, Prussia (now a part of Poland), on December 19, 1852. When he was two years old, his family moved to the United States, and he became an American citizen. In 1869, President Ulysses S. Grant appointed Michelson to the United States Naval Academy in Annapolis, Maryland, and he graduated four years later. In 1875, he became a science instructor at the Naval Academy, and his clarity and precision were well noted. He stayed in the navy performing various missions but got a leave of absence to study physics in Europe. A short while later, he resigned from the navy and in 1883 accepted a position as a professor of physics at the Case School of Applied Science in Cleveland, Ohio. In 1890, he moved to Clark University in Worcester, Massachusetts, and then was honored to become the first department head of physics at the new University of Chicago in 1892.

Rejoining the navy during World War I, Michelson engaged in researching and developing various military devices such as a rangefinder, used for determining the distance and position of an enemy ship. At the end of the war, he returned to Chicago.

Albert Michelson, shown here as a young man in his naval uniform (AIP Emilio Segrè Visual Archives)

Because the speed of light is enormous and its wavelength so small, optical measurements have little room for error and require a delicate touch. Michelson excelled at this kind of measurement and prided himself on continually improving his precision throughout his career. In 1920, he became interested in astronomy and used an interferometer to make the first accurate determination of the diameter of a star (Betelgeuse). He continued working until the end of his life, dying at age 78 in 1931.

This photo shows the arms of an interferometer, used by Albert Michelson's colleague Edward Morley and a coworker to study the speed of light in the presumed ether as the beams traveled along the arms. [AIP Emilio Segrè Visual Archives]

electromagnetic waves, which they called the ether. Michelson thought to study the ether by showing how it slows down light. He assumed, as did all scientists at the time, that the velocity of a beam of light on Earth would be greater in the direction that the planet was traveling. The reason for this is that velocities appear to add. If a person walking at three miles per hour (4.8 km/hr) steps onto a conveyor belt moving at five miles per hour (8 km/hr), the speed of the person is the sum of both speeds, eight miles per hour (12.8 km/hr), relative to the ground.

Michelson and Morley set up their interferometer so that one beam of light traveled in the same direction Earth is moving and the other beam traveled at right angles to this direction. The first beam should have a higher velocity—the speed of light plus the speed of Earth—and when the two beams travel equal distances and meet, their different phases should have produced interference fringes. But the experimenters saw no fringes, so the beams must have made the trip in the same amount of time. This experiment, called the Michelson-Morley experiment, indicated that the speed of light is constant and does not increase with the motion of other objects.

By following the light, scientists had made many discoveries. Light is an electromagnetic wave that propagates through space at a certain velocity. But the Michelson-Morley experiment showed a curious feature of light, and, as described in the next chapter, the explanation for this experiment, along with further discoveries, would add even more curious and interesting facts.

4

LIGHT SURPRISES

In 1868, two astronomers, Pierre-Jules-César Janssen and Sir Joseph Norman Lockyer, independently discovered a new element. The substance proved to be the second most abundant element in the universe (after hydrogen), but very little exists on Earth. This is why astronomers were the ones who first found it—they made the discovery while examining light from the Sun. They called the element helium, after the Greek word for Sun, *helios*.

Light had plenty of surprises in store for scientists in the 19th and early 20th centuries. As described in the preceding chapter, the experiments and theories of Thomas Young, James Clerk Maxwell, and Heinrich Hertz showed that light is an electromagnetic wave, contrary to the belief of many scientists at the time. But problems cropped up with the notion of light as a wave because light had strange and unusual properties. For example, the Michelson-Morley experiment, also discussed in the previous chapter, suggested that light has a constant velocity no matter what the speed of the source. Light emitted from a stationary flashlight has the same speed as light emitted from a rocket traveling at thousands of miles per hour.

Astronomers noted another interesting aspect of light when they turned their instruments to the Sun and stars. Newton used prisms to prove that light consists of a spectrum, and astronomers in the early 1800s found that the spectrum of sunlight and starlight had distinct gaps. These gaps appeared as narrow dark lines in the spectrum, as if something was absorbing light at those particular regions. Only after studying these lines did astronomers realize they now had a tool to identify elements and compounds all over the universe.

Analyzing the Spectrum

The founder of *spectroscopy* was Joseph von Fraunhofer (1787–1826). Spectroscopy is the study of spectra (plural of spectrum), and as a young man, Fraunhofer noticed that the light from the Sun, when spread into its spectrum, was not a continuous band of color since it was missing some of the frequencies. These dark lines had been seen before by William Wollaston, but in 1814, Fraunhofer made a more detailed set of observations and found about 600 dark lines, many of

Joseph von Fraunhofer (1787–1826)—Biography

If a house had not collapsed and buried young Fraunhofer in a pile of rubble, the history of optics would have been much different. The accident was lucky in two ways: Fraunhofer was not seriously injured, and the man on hand when the boy was rescued was none other than Prince Maximilian Joseph—later King Max.

Fraunhofer was born in Bavaria on March 6, 1787. Although he loved to read, as a boy Fraunhofer had no time for study. Orphaned at age 11, he supported himself by working as an apprentice to a glassmaker. He was 14 when, in 1801, the building collapsed. The prince offered to help and made sure that Fraunhofer had the time and money to pursue his studies. Fraunhofer received instruction in the craft of optical instruments, and his determination and abilities—which had not been encouraged during his earlier apprenticeship—drove him to excel. At 22 years of age, he found himself appointed as the manager of a glass factory. Under Fraunhofer, the company was highly successful, producing optical instruments of superior quality and precision. These products were admired and used throughout Europe.

Using the instruments himself, Fraunhofer won praise for the carefulness and accuracy of his optical measurements. The tools and the diligence with which he used them enabled the formerly poor apprentice to which he measured. He gave the lines names such as D_1, identifiers that astronomers often still use today. Although Fraunhofer did not realize it, this was the first monumental step toward understanding the composition of the distant Sun and stars.

The Sun and stars are so remote that many people in the 19th century believed that no one would ever determine their composition. Even years after Fraunhofer's discovery, in the middle of the 19th century, the famous French philosopher Auguste Comte predicted that star composition would remain forever beyond human knowledge. A few decades later, he was proved wrong when the German scientists Robert Bunsen (1811–99) and Gustav Kirchhoff (1824–87) found that the dark spectral lines corresponded to frequencies where light was absorbed by specific elements.

conduct the spectroscopic studies that made him famous. Fraunhofer's work laid the groundwork for spectroscopic studies, which today are frequently used in many scientific fields such as chemistry, biology, and astronomy. By studying the spectroscopic properties of materials, scientists can determine the identify of substances and the structure of its molecules. Astronomers can even study the composition of the Sun and other stars, even though stars besides the Sun are far too distant to visit.

Joseph von Fraunhofer pioneered the study of the spectrum of astronomical objects such as the Sun. (AIP Emilio Segrè Visual Archives, W. F. Meggers Collection)

The king of Bavaria knighted him in 1824 for his service to science and optics, giving Fraunhofer the right to use *von* in his name (a title of nobility, similar to *sir* in England). Fraunhofer's life was tragically cut short by tuberculosis on June 7, 1826.

Joseph von Fraunhofer developed instruments such as this spectrometer, used to spread light into its components frequencies. [AIP Emilio Segrè Visual Archives]

Atoms emit and absorb electromagnetic waves when electrons change from one orbit to another, as discussed in chapter 1. The frequency of electromagnetic waves determines its energy—higher frequencies have higher energies—and atoms absorb specific amounts of energy. The amount of energy is exactly what is required to lift an electron into one of its many possible high-energy orbits. Since the electrons of different atoms have different orbits, each atomic element absorbs its own unique set of frequencies. An atom of helium, for example, absorbs light at frequencies of 511 trillion Hertz, 598 trillion Hertz, 671 trillion Hertz, and many others.

The lines Fraunhofer observed are the spectral frequencies of light absorbed by the elements in the Sun. Electromagnetic waves arising in the interior of the Sun pass through its gaseous outer layers, where the elements absorb their specific frequencies. (Eventually the atoms emit this light, but because the radiated energy spreads in all directions, most of it escapes the original light beam.) Analyzing the spectra of the Sun, stars, and galaxies gave astronomers a tool to determine the chemical composition of these distant objects.

After analyzing a large number of spectra, astronomers began to classify stars based on their spectrum. A small number of categories emerged—there were patterns of absorption lines, and most stars fit into one or another of these categories. Scientists soon realized that these categories were related to the temperature of the surface of the star, providing yet more information. Designations of standard types of stars are O, B, A, F, G, K, and M, and the categories are subdivided into numbers 0–9. (The Sun is a G2 star.) This classification gave astronomers a better understanding of how stars form and how they spend millions or billions of years shining brightly. Developing the classification required a tremendous effort because a huge number of stars had to be analyzed. The responsibility for most of this work fell squarely on the shoulders of a dedicated team of female astronomers at the Harvard College Observatory. "The Harvard Astronomers" sidebar gives some information on this remarkable group of women.

An absorption spectrum is due to atomic electrons absorbing certain frequencies out of the light traveling through a gas, but in the 19th

Before the invention of calculators and computers, mathematics had to be done by hand, as by these female "computers" at Harvard College Observatory. [Harvard College Observatory, AIP Emilio Segrè Visual Archives]

The Harvard Astronomers—Biography

Before the 20th century, most people did not often encourage women to choose science as a career. In the 1900s, this began to change, and the work of the Harvard Astronomers—especially Annie J. Cannon (1863–1941), Antonia Maury (1866–1952), and Williamina Fleming (1857–1911)—showed how women can be scientifically productive. These women made many of the observations and did much of the analysis leading to the spectral classification system used by astronomers today.

Members of the team of astronomers at Harvard College Observatory, holding hands and standing in front of the building. Annie J. Cannon is fifth from right. [Harvard College Observatory, AIP Emilio Segrè Visual Archives]

century, scientists did not quite understand this process. They believed light was an electromagnetic wave, and scientists could not comprehend how or why an atom's electrons absorbed specific frequencies, instead of absorbing light of all frequencies. One of the physicists who came up with an explanation for this process was Albert Einstein (1879–1955)—but his theory caused a major revision in the way scientists perceive and understand light.

Albert Einstein and the Photoelectric Effect

Early in his career, Einstein became interested in light, and he greatly admired the work of James Clerk Maxwell, who a few decades before

Annie J. Cannon spent her childhood star-gazing, and she obtained a physics degree from Wellesley College in Massachusetts in 1884. Career options for women at the time were limited, so Cannon struggled to find decent work. A severe hearing loss contributed to her difficulties. After coming to Radcliffe women's college at Harvard College, she accepted a position as an assistant at Harvard's observatory in 1896. She worked under the supervision of Professor Edward C. Pickering. She spent most of her career at Harvard, cataloging more than 200,000 spectra by the early 20th century and ordering the stars into standard spectra types.

Antonia Maury was the niece of prominent astronomer Henry Draper and graduated from Vassar College, New York, in 1887. Like Cannon, she found work at Harvard College Observatory during the enormous effort of gathering and sorting a huge number of astronomical observations. Her classification system was ahead of its time, and she argued with some of the professors, but her work was gradually accepted and used in charting the lifetime and evolution of stars.

Perhaps the most interesting of the women is Williamina Fleming. In 1881, she was a maid at the home of Professor Pickering. One day, Pickering fired one of his assistants, declaring that anyone could do a better job. To prove it, Pickering hired his maid. She turned out to be extremely efficient at the task, and over the years, she cataloged thousands of stars and supervised the work of many of the women at the Harvard College Observatory.

Einstein had hypothesized that light is an electromagnetic wave. One of Einstein's first scientific papers dealt with the speed of light, which Einstein claimed was constant—in accordance with the findings of the Michelson-Morley experiment, described in the previous chapter. Using this as a basis, Einstein deduced numerous consequences, many of which were striking. Because the speed of light was constant, Einstein showed how time and simultaneity—the relative time of events—depend on the observer's speed. These ideas formed the theory of relativity and made Einstein famous.

Einstein's interest in light led him to consider the photoelectric effect. The German physicist Heinrich Hertz noted in 1887 that *ultraviolet* light—an invisible form of electromagnetic waves with frequencies slightly higher than visible light—caused a current to flow when it struck the surface of a metal. The energy of the ultraviolet light was sufficient to knock electrons completely out of the orbit of the metal's

Albert Einstein (1879–1955)—Biography

Born in Ulm, Germany, in March 14, 1879, Einstein's early life did not show much evidence that he would go on to become one of the world's greatest physicists. His teachers considered him a slow learner—probably due to his difficulties with language—and 19th-century Germany was a rigid and militaristic society, not suited to the free-spirited nature of young Einstein. As a rebellious teenager, Einstein's future did not look bright.

Although hardly a model pupil, Einstein did begin to show promise in mathematics and science. In 1901, he obtained a physics degree from the Swiss Federal Polytechnic School in Zurich and became a citizen of Switzerland. His diploma meant that he could become a teacher, but his argumentative and disruptive nature caused one of his college professors to give him a bad reference so no school hired him. Instead, Einstein took a job as a clerk in the Swiss Patent Office in 1902. During his spare time, he continued to think about physics, and it was during these years that Einstein's brilliance really shined. In 1905, he published papers on the theory of relativity, photons of light, and a study of the random motion of molecules. Any one of these papers would have established a solid reputation, and together they proved to be the work of a genius. In 1921, Einstein received the Nobel Prize in physics.

After earning a doctorate, Einstein obtained professorships in Switzerland and Germany, and in 1914, he became the director of the Kaiser Wilhelm Physical Institute and a professor at the University of Berlin. He continued his excellent theoretical work in physics, improving upon Newton's law of universal gravitation. When Hitler and the Nazis rose to power in Germany in 1933, Einstein—who would have been persecuted under the Nazi regime because he was a Jew—was visiting the United States. He decided to stay in this country and accepted a position at Princeton University in New Jersey. Einstein remained there for the rest of his life, working on advanced problems in physics and warning the U.S. government on the possibility of an atomic bomb—which, like most of this brilliant physicist's statements, proved accurate.

Einstein died on April 18, 1955, at Princeton, New Jersey.

atoms, and the negatively charged particles flew away. The mystery was why ultraviolet light was necessary. If light is an electromagnetic wave, then shining any frequency on the metal should eventually liberate an electron because the atomic electrons should absorb enough light to leave their orbits after a while. But this is not what happened. Only light of a certain frequency liberated the electrons, and they began to fly off at once when the light switched on.

Einstein explained the photoelectric effect in 1905 by proposing the existence of a particle of light called the *photon*. Light comes in a stream of photons, said Einstein—similar to the old hypothesis of Newton—and when an atomic electron in the metal absorbs a photon with enough energy, the electron is kicked out of orbit. A photon's energy is proportional to its "frequency," and only higher-frequency light has enough energy to remove the electrons. Although Einstein's idea was revolutionary, it fit well with other, new theories, such as that developed by the German physicist Max Planck (1858–1947). Planck had proposed in 1900 that energy is not continuous but comes in a packet, or quantum. Einstein's photons were quickly accepted as real, and the citation for his 1921 Nobel Prize in physics mentions Einstein's explanation for the photoelectric effect as deserving special merit.

But Einstein's idea raised a puzzling difficulty. Young, Maxwell, and Hertz had shown that light is an electromagnetic wave—and this is an entirely different phenomenon from a particle.

Particles and Waves

A particle is a discrete object, occupying some small but specific space. A wave is a periodic motion through a medium. A person can imagine a particle, such as a grain of sand, and can imagine a wave, such as ripples on a pond—but no one can imagine anything that is both a wave and a particle.

Yet light seemed to be just that. Young's double-slit experiment and Maxwell's equations, described in chapter 3, confirmed the wave properties of light. Einstein's photons showed their particle properties. Danish physicist Niels Bohr (1885–1962) used both wave and particle properties when he devised a model of the hydrogen atom in which electrons occupied only certain orbits. Electrons absorb photons as they move to a higher-energy orbit and emit photons when they fall to a lower one. Bohr's model explained the spectrum because it predicted the correct frequencies for the spectral lines, and Bohr won the 1922 Nobel Prize in physics.

But it was impossible for physicists to understand how something can be both a wave and a particle, and they were upset over talk of a photon's "frequency" or "wavelength." Then scientists discovered that even particles like electrons have a wavelength, so wave-particle duality must be true.

Going back to Young's double-slit experiment, physicists used weak sources of light so that only a few photons would travel through one of the slits; they wondered what would happen under those conditions to the interference pattern, with which Young had proved that light was a wave. What happened is that the interference fringes developed gradually—even though only one or two photons passed through the slits at a time. The photons interfered with themselves!

For now, physicists and optical scientists must accept wave-particle duality. Sometimes light acts like wave; sometimes it acts like a particle. But the strangeness of this concept makes some people wonder whether the current scientific understanding is the final explanation, or whether future research may reveal an even deeper level. Light may have further surprises in store for those who dare to study it.

5

MIRRORS AND LENSES

Optical instruments are tools to bend and guide light. The most basic of these tools are mirrors and lenses, which have been used since the days of ancient Greece and Rome, as described in chapter 2. They are simple yet powerful devices, and although Archimedes may not have actually built a set of burning mirrors, people used glass and metal to start small fires with the Sun or to signal each other over long distances.

Discovering the scientific laws that govern these simple instruments was not so easy, except in the case of a plane (flat) mirror. Curved mirrors and lenses displayed more complex behavior, and constructing glass or metal objects in a functional shape required a great deal of skill—more than 1,000 years passed between the time that the ancient Greek scientist Ptolemy wrote about optical magnification and the appearance of the first eyeglasses. What the early optical scientists and engineers needed to learn were the rules by which mirrors change the direction of light and the rules by which glass slows light down.

Mirrors: Bouncing Light

The law of reflection has been known at least since the ancient Greek philosopher Euclid. Euclid treated the study of light geometrically; in his diagrams, he drew light as lines called rays. Today people describe

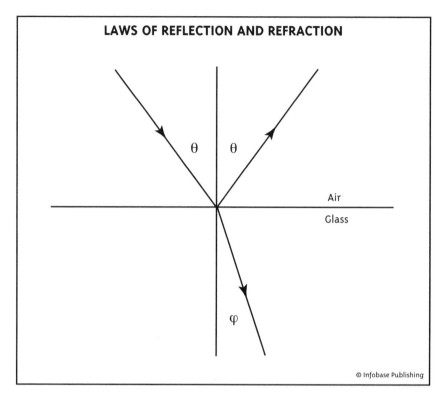

LAWS OF REFLECTION AND REFRACTION

Air

Glass

© Infobase Publishing

The top part of the figure illustrates the law of reflection: A light ray traveling in air strikes the surface of the glass at angle θ and reflects at an equal angle. The bottom part of the figure shows the path of a light ray that passes from the air into the glass; the ray refracts and makes an angle φ with the normal. The angle φ is less than θ in this situation, but the opposite is true when light travels from glass into air.

the behavior of mirrors and lenses in the same way, and this subject forms a branch of optics called *geometrical optics.*

The law of reflection states that light rays reflect from a surface at the same angle at which they strike. The surface can be any object—all objects reflect at least a little light, including glass—and the surface can be in any shape, though the law is easiest to observe when the surface is flat, as shown in the figure. By convention, angles are measured relative to the perpendicular of the surface, called the normal.

Most mirrors are flat surfaces. Early mirrors were made of a thin sheet of metal, but today they are usually a thin coating of aluminum on the back of a plate of transparent glass. Not just any surface will do for a mirror—all objects reflect light, but only a few, such as metal, glass, and the calm surface of a body of water, make good mirrors.

The essential property is smoothness: A mirror must be so smooth that even the tiny wavelengths of light bounce off in an orderly fashion. An image forms only when the reflected light does not scatter; the rays of a person's reflection, for example, must stay together so that the light from the lips remain above the chin and beneath the nose instead of scattering all over. The wavelength of visible light ranges from 0.000016–0.000027 inches (400–700 nanometers [nm]), so the mirror must be smooth down to this incredibly small level. A piece of paper seems smooth to a person's touch, but it is not smooth on the level of visible light, so the paper scatters light and does not make a functional mirror.

Curved mirrors can be useful because, if they have the right shape, they can collect and focus the light onto a point, called the *focal point.* Light bouncing off a curved surface obeys the law of reflection, but for a *concave mirror*—inward-curving—the light bounces toward the midline. If the mirror has a paraboloid shape, as described in chapter 2, then parallel rays of light *converge* to the focal point, as shown in part (a) of the figure on page 41. This kind of mirror is useful because it focuses light.

The calm water of the Schuylkill River in Philadelphia, Pennsylvania, makes a good mirror, reflecting light from the buildings along its bank. (Kyle Kirkland)

The choppy water of the Delaware River near Philadelphia, Pennsylvania, shimmers as it reflects sunlight from its waves. Clear images do not form when the surface is wavy and uneven. [Kyle Kirkland]

A paraboloid is a difficult shape, and often manufacturers use a simpler shape—a section of a sphere. Spherical mirrors do not focus as crisply as a paraboloid, but they work well enough, except for precision work such as telescopes (which are discussed in chapter 8). For an outward-curving, *convex mirror*, all the light reflects away from the midline, as shown in part (b) of the figure. The diverging rays all appear to come from some point behind the mirror; this point is also called the focal point.

Lenses: Focusing Light

Whereas mirrors form an image by changing the direction of light, lenses form an image by bending light. But refraction is much more complicated than reflection. Most historians credit the discovery of the law of refraction to a Dutchman, Willebrod Snell (1591–1626), in 1621, but Snell did not publish much of his ideas, and there is some doubt as to who actually made this discovery and when.

Materials such as glass bend light because light slows down when traveling through a substance. Although the speed of light is constant, as Einstein and the Michelson-Morley experiment showed, it is constant only for a given material—light has a different speed in air, water, and glass. The speed of light in a substance is slower than in a vacuum; in empty space, light propagates without interacting with matter, but

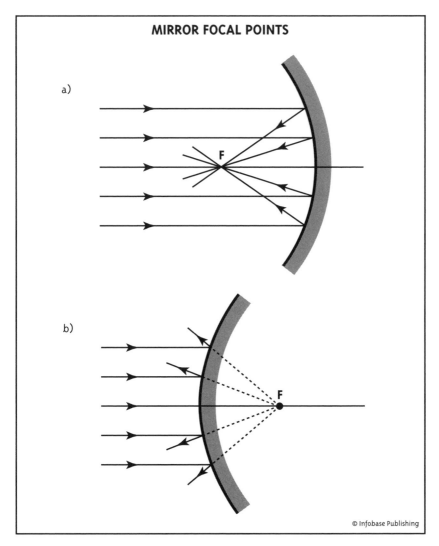

MIRROR FOCAL POINTS

(a) The light rays come from a distant object and are parallel. *F* is the focal point of the concave mirror. (b) The focal point of a convex mirror is behind the reflecting surface. Light rays reflect away from the midline.

when light travels through matter, it engages atoms and other particles that resist its motion.

Refraction of light occurs when light passes from one material (or a vacuum) to a different material at some angle greater than zero. The *interface* between two different materials, or between a vacuum and a substance, is where light bends. The bending is due to the slowing down of one part of the wave front before the rest, and this occurs when light strikes the interface at an angle other than perpendicular (which is 0°, as measured relative to the normal). The figure on page 43 shows a wave front encountering an interface; one ray is drawn, and the solid lines perpendicular to the ray represent the crests of the light waves that are propagating together. The change in speed does not occur along the wave front at the same time, so the wave gets twisted. In the top part of the figure, the light goes from a material in which it travels quickly to a material in which it moves more slowly, and in the bottom, it does the opposite, from slow to fast. The bending is in different directions.

The amount of bending depends on how much the speed of light changes. The speed of light in a vacuum divided by the speed of light through a particular material is that material's *index of refraction.* Since matter tends to reduce the speed of light, the index of refraction is generally a number greater than 1.0. The index of refraction for air is 1.0003—light travels in air almost as quickly as in empty space—but for water, the index of refraction is 1.33, and for many types of glass, it is about 1.5.

When light travels from a material with a low index of refraction to a material with a higher one, the light bends toward the normal, as illustrated in the figure on page 38; when traveling from a high index of refraction to low one, it bends the other way. The law of refraction determines how much light is bent by giving an equation relating θ_i, the angle the original ray makes (called the angle of incidence), and θ_r, the angle of the refracted ray. The equation uses trigonometric functions:

$$n_i \sin \theta_i = n_r \sin \theta_r,$$

where n_i is the index of refraction for the material that the light leaves, and n_r is the index of refraction for the material it enters. Trigonometry was not well understood until the Renaissance, and this delayed the discovery of this law. Ptolemy, the ancient Greek scientist, deduced an approximation for the law of refraction, but it worked only for small angles.

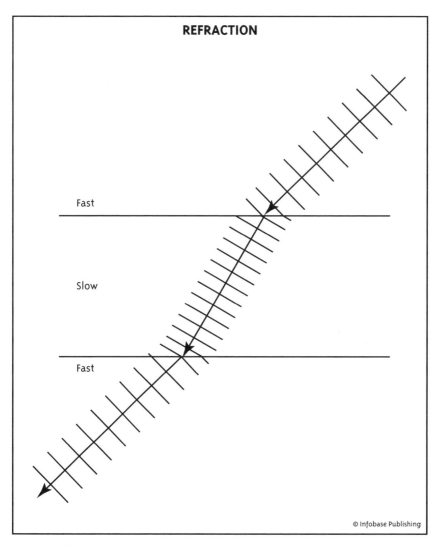

REFRACTION

Fast

Slow

Fast

© Infobase Publishing

Waves bend as they make a transition from one speed to another.

People construct lenses to take advantage of refraction: Lenses bend and focus light. The first lenses for eyeglasses appeared in the 13th century, preceding the discovery of the law of refraction. These lenses were made by trial and error, adding to the cost and reducing their effectiveness. Snell's law gave lens grinders a tool to perfect their craft.

A lens is made of a transparent substance such as glass that is carefully grinded to the correct shape. A *convex lens*, shown in the figure below, is thicker in the middle than at the edges (like a convex mirror).

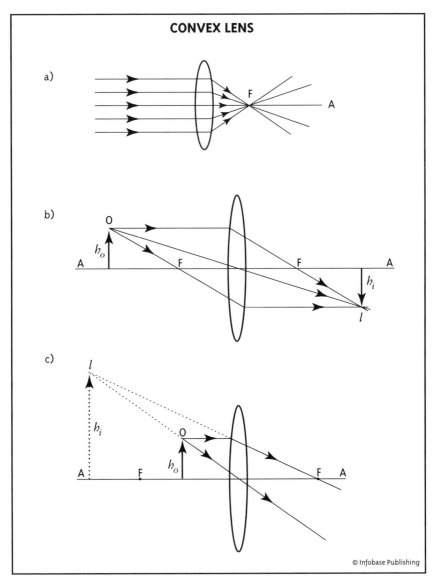

CONVEX LENS

a)

b)

c)

© Infobase Publishing

(a) Parallel rays converge to the focal point, *F*, of a convex lens. (b) An object h_o beyond the focal point makes an inverted, real image, h_i. (c) An object h_o closer to the lens than the focal point forms a magnified, virtual image h_i.

Light rays are bent twice, once entering the lens (the air-to-glass interface) and once exiting (the glass-to-air interface). Part (a) of the figure shows that parallel rays converge to a point called the focal point, similar to what happens with a mirror. The *focal length* is the distance from the lens to the focal point, and different lenses have different focal lengths, depending on the glass and the shape of the lens.

Light rays coming from an object move out in space in all directions, as seen in part (b) of the figure. A convex lens uses its refractive power to focus these rays and form an image. If the object is farther away from the lens than its focal length F, the rays from each point of the object converge to form an upside-down image, as shown in (b). This image is called a *real image*. Only three rays from a single point of the object are shown in the figure, but in reality, many rays come from all points.

Another type of image is a *virtual image*. Rays of light do not actually converge in a virtual image—they only appear to do so. Part (c) of the figure shows a virtual image formed by an object, indicated by the solid arrow, that is located closer to a convex lens than its focal length. Light from the object refracts, and because of the object's location, the rays *diverge*. But the divergence causes these rays to appear as if they were coming from object indicated by the dotted line. This image, a virtual image, is right-side up and magnified. When a person holds a convex lens close to an object, a large virtual image appears—convex lenses make good magnifying lenses, as the fictional detective Sherlock Holmes well knew.

Convex mirrors produce virtual images. Unlike a real image, a virtual image cannot be projected onto a screen—the image is not really present except in the eye of the beholder. People view the diverging rays as if they had really come straight from an object, although what actually happened is that the rays were bent. Convex mirrors offer a broad field of view and are often used in places where people need to see a wide area, such as behind a car in which they are driving. But the reflection seems to come from behind the mirror; the image looks smaller, and therefore the object appears to be farther away than it really is (which accounts for the warning on convex mirrors that objects are closer than they appear).

A concave lens, shown in the figure on page 46, is thinner in the middle. Because of its shape, concave lenses diverge light rays. All images formed by these lenses are virtual.

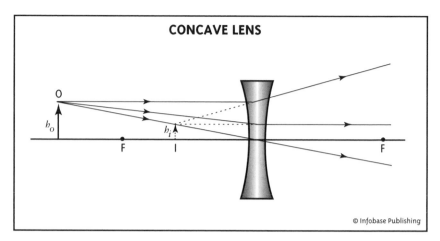

A concave lens refracts the light rays from an object h_o and forms a virtual image h_i.

Prisms: Bending Light

The index of refraction is usually given as a single number, but it actually depends on a specific property of light, the frequency (or wavelength). Glass, for instance, bends light with a higher frequency (shorter wavelength) slightly more than light with a lesser frequency. As a result, glass spreads light out into its spectrum, a phenomenon called *dispersion*.

Triangular-shaped glass, a prism, is an excellent tool to demonstrate dispersion. The figure on page 47 illustrates the process. Newton and other early physicists used prisms to spread white light into its frequency spectrum and study the components.

But a prism is not the only material that shows dispersion. Since the index of refraction of glass has a dependence on frequency, lenses act as prisms as well. This means that an ordinary convex lens will not be able to bring all the light from an object into focus because light at different frequencies will not bend the same amount and therefore will fail to converge. The deficiency is usually small, but in precision optical instruments, it is noticeable and most unwelcome. The result is a blurry image suffering from what is called *chromatic aberration*. The solution for chromatic aberration involves an expensive combination of different glasses and coatings to smooth out the index of refraction for the lens.

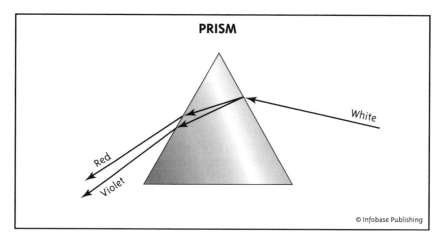

PRISM

White

Red

Violet

© Infobase Publishing

Because refraction depends on wavelength, a glass prism spreads white light into its color spectrum.

Chromatic aberration gets its name because it is a deviation or derangement (aberration) of color. The color comes from the dispersion. People see different frequencies (wavelengths) as different colors, and so the spectrum displayed by a prism is colorful. But colors show up everywhere, not just from glass prisms and lenses. The following chapter takes a closer look at colors, and chapter 7 explains how people see them.

THE COLORS OF LIGHT

Although Sir Isaac Newton's experiments with prisms showed that sunlight—white, uncolored light—is a mixture of colors, not everyone believed him. People today regard Newton's experiments as conclusive, but writers and philosophers such as the great German poet Johann Wolfgang von Goethe refused to accept the idea. Colored light was difficult to understand—colors seemed to belong to objects, such as a red apple or the blue sky. To artists, colors meant paint and *pigments*.

But Newton was correct. White light is uncolored, but it is a mixture—a sum of all the colors of the spectrum. The dispersion of prisms reveals the spectrum, as does a rainbow, a natural phenomenon often seen in the sky after a morning or afternoon rain shower. Colors are everywhere, on flowers, ripe fruit, and animals. Light is the sole provider of color on the ground and in the sky, and every object gets its color because it emits, refracts, reflects, or scatters a portion of the spectrum of light. The basis for the spectrum is wavelength.

Wavelength and Color

Wavelength λ and frequency f are related by the equation

$$\lambda f = c,$$

where c is the speed of the wave. So although many optical scientists talk about wavelength and color, a related property, frequency, could

These flowers add beauty to Fairmount Park, in Philadelphia, Pennsylvania. [Kyle Kirkland]

also serve. And because of wave-particle duality, photons can be said to have a wavelength, frequency, and color—but when it comes to color, most people prefer to think of light as a wave.

Prisms spread white light into its component wavelengths, which as discussed in the following chapter are perceived by the human visual system as colors. But colored objects such as an apple do not spread out light. An apple is red because of selective absorption: It absorbs more of all other wavelengths of the spectrum than for a range of wavelengths about 0.000026 inches (650 nm), which is mostly reflected. These reflected wavelengths are what people see when they look at an apple, and the visual system interprets this range of wavelength as red. All objects absorb some light falling on them and reflect the rest, and most objects—except white ones—are better at absorbing certain wavelengths than others. An object that reflects mostly shorter wavelengths (higher frequencies) appears blue or violet, and an object that reflects mostly the mid-range appears greenish. Mixtures of wavelengths produce more colors; there are millions of different possibilities, although people cannot distinguish quite that many.

Adding together all the colors of light makes white—a difficult concept for artists since combining all the paints on a palette results in a dark, muddy brown. Combining paint is different than combining light because the color of paint, like other colored objects and unlike light, is one of reflection and absorption. Mixing light means adding wavelengths, but mixing paints means taking them away—one paint absorbs a certain range of wavelengths, and the other paint absorbs a different set. The remaining wavelengths that are reflected produce the mixture's color; when the mixture consists of many different colors combined together, there is little light reflected, and the result is a dark color. Chapter 17 discusses paints in more detail.

Light is generally a mixture of wavelengths, and when one or a few are prominent, the light is colored. Sunlight consists of an approximately equal mixture of the visible wavelengths and so it is not colored, but in artificial lights the mixture is not so equal. Fluorescent lightbulbs generally emit more of the shorter wavelengths, so it appears slightly bluish. This means a white object—one that reflects all wavelengths equally—will have a bluish tint under fluorescent lighting. Although fluorescent lighting is efficient, it does not flatter the skin tones of Caucasian and other fair-skinned peoples since it tends to make them look unhealthy. Candlelight, on the other hand, with its reddish orange glow, makes fair-skinned peoples appear radiant and healthy—just the thing for a romantic dinner.

Color of the Sky

Perhaps the most noticeable colored object is the sky. Like all colors, the blue of the sky comes from a portion of the electromagnetic spectrum—the shorter wavelengths of visible light. But the process is different: The sky is blue because air molecules scatter short wavelengths.

Light from the sky comes from the Sun, but it appears colored because of the air. The Moon lacks an atmosphere, and its sky is black, as observed by the Apollo astronauts. In the Moon's sky, the Sun is a big glowing object surrounded by darkness. On Earth, the air molecules of the atmosphere scatter light, throwing it out of the direct beam of the Sun; when people on this planet look up during the day, they see light in all directions. (The Sun should not be viewed directly, though, since its brightness will damage unprotected eyes.) This light is blue because the Earth's atmosphere selectively scatters shorter wavelengths. As the Sun's rays travel through the atmosphere, they encounter air molecules that absorb and reemit light—the longer wavelengths (red) pass through without much trouble, but the blue gets sidetracked. The short wavelengths of visible light get bounced from one molecule to the next, zigzagging down to finally reach the ground from all directions.

Sunsets and sunrises are red instead of blue, but the reason is the same. During the middle of the day, the Sun is directly overhead, and the light does not have to pass through much of the atmosphere to reach the people below. In the morning or evening, the Sun is low on the horizon, and the sunlight skims over the surface of the planet, traveling through a large quantity of air until it reaches the eye of the viewer. The atmosphere scatters out a lot of the blue light along the way, so the light people see during sunset and sunrise has a deficiency in the shorter wavelengths and an excess of the longer one. The result is a reddish-orange color—the color of sunsets and sunrises.

Dust can also scatter light. A dirty, polluted atmosphere tends to scatter more light, so sunsets are prettier and more colorful, though this is small compensation for foul air. Volcanoes emit huge amounts of ash, dust, and gases, some of which can travel for great distances and stay in the atmosphere for weeks or even months. The gigantic explosion of the Indonesian island of Krakatau, in 1883, sent tons of debris in the air. Sunsets were exceptionally colored for years afterward.

This photograph captured a New Mexico sunset. [Kyle Kirkland]

   The sky of other worlds does not have to be similar to Earth's. The Moon's sky is black, but even a planet with an atmosphere need not have the familiar blue sky of this planet. Mars has a thin atmosphere of mostly carbon dioxide. Probes such as those used during the Viking missions of the 1970s and with the Mars rovers *Spirit* and *Opportunity* in 2004 and 2005 sent back pictures of a barren, desolate surface under a yellowish brown or sometimes salmon-colored sky, depending on the amount of dust.

Rainbows

One feature of light that remains the same on all planets throughout the universe is the spectrum of visible light. Prisms always yield the same colors. So do rainbows and for a similar reason. While the glass of a prism produces the dispersion that spreads out light into its spectrum, in a rainbow this task belongs to tiny droplets of water.

This rainbow appeared as a fitting tribute to Sir Isaac Newton at his birthplace, Woolsthorpe, England. (AIP Emilio Segrè Visual Archives)

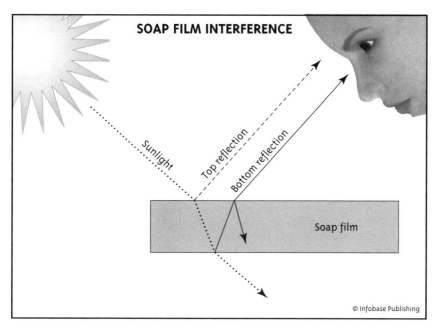

Light waves reflecting from the top and bottom of the soap film travel slightly different distances to the observer and interfere with each other.

Rainbows in their full splendor are circular, although on most occasions people glimpse only an arc. Water drops are spherical, suspended in the air by winds and storms, and reflect some of the light passing through them. Reflection occurs at all interfaces—any time two materials meet, part of the light will be transmitted (and refracted), and part of the light will be reflected. Light traveling through a water drop encounters two interfaces, one going in and one going out. Both interfaces reflect some of the light—perhaps 5 percent or so of the total—and the light that bounces off the rear wall and passes back through the front is refracted. The effect is the same as a prism because water slows down violet light about 1 percent more than red light. The colors of the spectrum separate, and a rainbow appears.

The best time to see a rainbow is after a morning or afternoon rain shower because water drops are plentiful and the Sun is not too high. Viewers should face away from the Sun; if the Sun's rays make an angle of about 42 degrees with the viewer's line of sight, a rainbow can be seen. The angle is necessary because the reflection from the spherical drops will be concentrated at this position, increasing one's chances of seeing one of nature's most colorful displays. But the water drops need not come from the weather—fountain spray will work just as well.

Colors also appear on soap bubbles and oil spills, though for a different reason. These colors are due to interference of light waves reflecting from thin films.

Soap bubbles have skins with a thickness of only about 1/250,000th of an inch (0.1 micrometer [µm]), and light bounces off both sides, inner and outer. The reflected rays from the inner side take a slightly different path than the outer because of the width of the bubble, as illustrated in the figure on page 53. This width is extremely short, but it makes a difference to light because of its tiny wavelengths. Similar to Young's double-slit experiment, described in chapter 3, these waves interfere. Some of the waves cancel and some do not, depending on the phase difference between them; when the waves are completely out of phase, the crest and trough aligns, and the wave disappears. Since the phase depends on wavelength, colors arise—light at some wavelengths cancels, but light at other wavelengths do not. Oil films and any other thin, transparent material exhibit the same situation. Light reflecting from the shiny side of a CD or DVD is also colored because of interference.

Reflection, refraction, absorption, scattering, and interference are behaviors of light as it interacts with itself and pieces of matter. Earth is a colorful place because of these interactions. But colors, or any light at all for that matter, could not be enjoyed without the sense of vision. The following chapter explains how people see.

7

HOW PEOPLE SEE: EYE AND VISION

Most animals have eyes, though few have eyes and vision as good as humans. (Other senses, such as smell, are more important to the survival of many species.) While spiders have six or eight eyes, this number does not give them three or four times better eyesight than people. The lens of a spider's eye is not adjustable, so the animal has a limited range of vision and must move its whole body to focus—imagine being able to recognize friends only if they are a certain distance away. Many spiders build webs to catch food and do not need great eyesight, but hunting spiders, such as the wolf spider, use their numerous eyes to scan a large area for prey. Some hunting spiders can even move their retinas, giving them a little extra flexibility in seeing the world.

The human eye and visual system are one of the most complex and remarkable systems in biology. Humans, monkeys, and apes generally have excellent vision. The visual system includes an adjustable lens to focus on objects near and far, the ability to see many different colors, and a brain that devotes about half its information-processing power to interpreting what is being seen. With all that complexity, many things can go wrong and often do. About 60 to 70 percent of the adult population requires some form of eyesight correction.

Vision begins with the eye. The eye transforms light into elec-trochemical signals that the brain uses to process information. Like a camera or microscope or any other instrument that uses light, the eye must have good optical properties in order to function.

Optics of the Eye

The figure below shows a drawing of the human eye. The most impor-tant parts concerning optics are the cornea, lens, pupil, and retina.

The focusing power of the eyes comes mostly from the cornea, the shape of which forms a lenslike object to bend and focus light. The lens of the eye is made from water and proteins. Despite its name, it does not provide much refraction, but it is critical because tiny mus-cles called ciliary muscles change the shape of the lens so that the eye

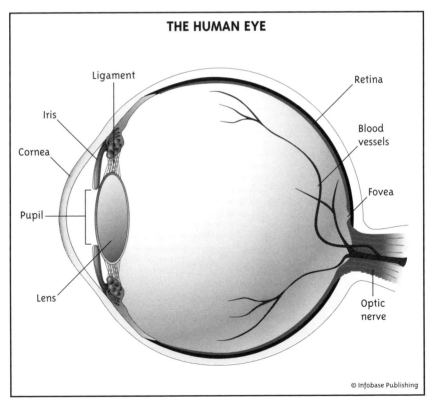

The anatomy of the human eye.

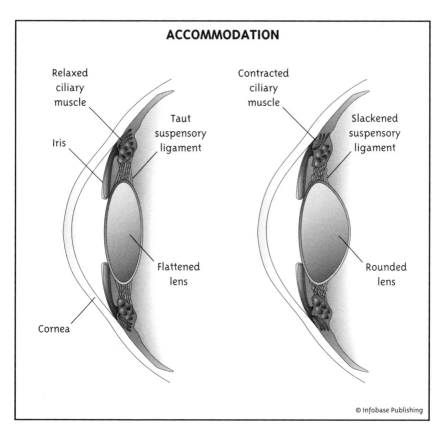

ACCOMMODATION

Relaxed ciliary muscle

Iris

Taut suspensory ligament

Flattened lens

Cornea

Contracted ciliary muscle

Slackened suspensory ligament

Rounded lens

© Infobase Publishing

Contraction or relaxation of the eye's ciliary muscles adjusts the tension on the ligaments holding the lens in place. The different shapes alter the refractory properties of the lens.

can undergo *accommodation*, the process of changing the focus. If the image is to be formed on a fixed screen (or retina), a lens of a given, unchanging shape can form a crisp image of objects located at only a small range of distances; the lens offers a fixed level of refraction, and the image of objects near or far forms at various locations behind the lens. A camera changes the focus by moving the lens (and if the lens cannot be moved, the picture-taker must move), but the human eye accommodates by changing the shape of its lens, as shown in the figure above. Forming an image of close objects requires more bending because their light rays are still spreading out when they reach the lens. To focus on close objects, the lens rounds up, increasing its bending power.

The eye of an adult human is roughly an inch (2.54 cm) in diameter. (Compare that to the size of a giant squid's eye, more than 10 inches [25 cm] across.) Light enters through a small hole called the pupil. The size of the pupil is important to control the amount of light—the pupil gets smaller, or constricts, on a sunny day because too much light can be blinding, and the pupil gets bigger, or dilates, at night to collect as much light as possible. The iris, the colored part of the eye, is a circular muscle that controls the size of the pupil.

Drugs can cause an inappropriate pupil response. Stimulants such as amphetamines and cocaine dilate the pupil, and people under the influence of these drugs often wear sunglasses in order to reduce the amount of light entering the eye (and to hide the telltale dilation). Heroin tends to constrict the pupil.

Nocturnal animals, including the cat, have a highly reflective layer of a substance called tapetum lucidum around the back of their eyes; these animals need to see at night, and the reflective layer bounces light around, giving the retina more chances to absorb it. But some light gets bounced out, so the eyes of these animals seem to glow at night when a flashlight shines on them.

The eight eyes of a spider can be arrayed to survey a large area from front to back, but both human eyes are placed to look straight ahead. On average, a person's eyes are 2.5 inches (6.3 cm) apart, and the reason there are two of them is to provide depth perception. Each eye gets a slightly different perspective, which can be seen by closing one eye and then the other—the visual scene appears to shift slightly. Closer objects shift more than ones farther away, and the brain uses this to calculate distance and depth. This binocular (two-eyed) vision provides a much better three-dimensional vision than a single eye could give.

Turning Light into Electrical Impulses

The task of the optics of the eye is to form an image on the retina. The job of the retina then becomes one of turning this image into something the brain can understand.

People sometimes have difficulty with this concept. Many people are so used to seeing with their "mind's eye" they forget there is no movie projector in the brain being watched by some little person—a

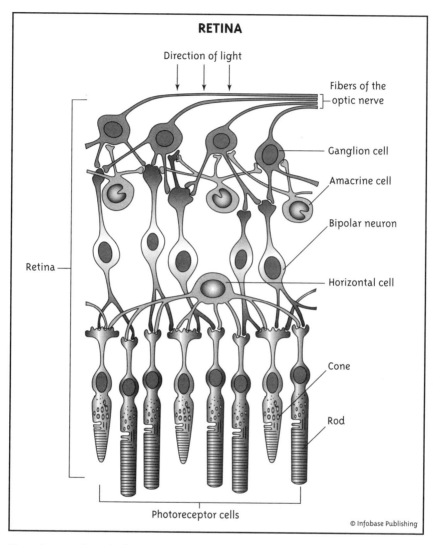

RETINA

Direction of light

Fibers of the optic nerve

Ganglion cell

Amacrine cell

Bipolar neuron

Retina

Horizontal cell

Cone

Rod

Photoreceptor cells

© Infobase Publishing

The retina consists of a large number of cells, including the rod and cone photoreceptors at the back. The horizontal, bipolar, amacrine, and ganglion cells process the signals from the photoreceptors and send the results to the visual part of the brain via the optic nerve. Light passes through the layers of cells, which are transparent, before being intercepted by the photoreceptors.

homunculus—who interprets the images. The human visual system relies on the cells called *photoreceptors* to transform light into impulses of electrical and chemical activity.

The retina is composed of several layers of cells. The photoreceptors are small cells with a diameter of about 0.000078–0.000195 inches (2–5 µm) that capture light waves and change this energy into impulses. (Biologists often prefer the particle designation for light, so photoreceptors are said to capture photons.) The human retina contains more than 100 million photoreceptors. The figure on page 59 displays a diagram of the retina and magnified views of the two main types of photoreceptor, rod and cone. The names are based on their shape, but this is not the only difference between the two.

In the photoreceptor are molecules that absorb light and change their form. Rod cells contain rhodopsin, consisting of two parts: an opsin molecule, which is a protein, and a molecule of retinal (made from vitamin A). Exposure to light splits rhodopsin into two parts, and this affects other molecules in the cell called ion channels that regulate the electrical activity of the cell. Ion channels allow charged particles, ions, into and out of the cell. Because of these ions, cells have an electric potential that varies, depending on how many ion channels are open. By affecting ion channels, the absorption of light signals its presence. The photoreceptors transmit this signal to other cells in the receptor by emitting small signaling molecules; these molecules influence ion channels in other cells, and the electrical signal passes from one cell to another through a chain of cells leading into the brain.

Rods are extremely sensitive to light. This sensitivity means they are effective in dim light, and rods provide night vision. Most of the photoreceptors in the retina are rods, and the majority of them are located away from the center. When a person stares at an object, the center of the gaze falls on the retina's *fovea*, an area packed with about 7 million cone photoreceptors and very few rods. The rods are in the periphery, so this is where a person's night vision excels. When looking at a faint star at night, it is best to direct the gaze a little to one side so that light from the star falls outside the fovea.

The fovea is relatively poor at night vision but is critical for seeing details. The rods in the periphery are linked together in broad networks. These cells act together so that they can magnify any light that happens to enter the eye, but as a result, peripheral vision is blurry—a person cannot see crisp images out of the corner of the eye. Cones in the fovea are not linked together and offer sharp vision with a lot of details—the fovea has fine *resolution*. To see small objects or details, a person looks directly at an object, and the image falls on the fovea.

The other job of the cones in the fovea is to detect colors.

Color Vision

Like rods, cones house light-absorbing molecules containing an opsin. But each cone has only one of three different types of opsins, so there are three types of cone. The opsins are tuned to a short range of wavelengths: There is a "red" cone, a "green" cone, and a "blue" cone, with each cone operating best when light of the corresponding wavelength strikes it.

Chapter 1 mentioned that the brain interprets signals from the retina as being visual simply because they are from the retina. This is called a labeled line process; knowing where a signal originated means knowing what it represents. Something similar happens with color vision. When a red cone sends a signal, the brain knows red light is present. The brain interprets blue and green cones similarly, and this is how the cone photoreceptors generate color vision.

There are only three different types of cone—red, green, and blue—yet people can see many different colors. Thomas Young was one of the first to offer an explanation for color vision based on three *primary colors*, though Young did not know anything about photoreceptors since they had not yet been discovered. Instead, Young based his ideas on the observation, described in the previous chapter, that lights of any color can be obtained by mixing three main, or primary, colors—he gave them as red, green, and violet.

Young's theory was not immediately accepted, and the German physiologist Ewald Hering (1834–1918) suggested that people see colors by an "opponent" process. Supporting Hering's ideas are phenomena such as complementary colors and afterimages. Two colors are complementary if they add to form white light; red and green are complementary, as are blue and yellow. Afterimages form when people stare at a color for a long time and then shift their gaze to a white sheet of paper, where a ghostly afterimage will briefly appear bearing the complementary color; for instance, staring at a red circle for a minute will produce on the blank sheet a faint but noticeable green circle that slowly fades.

Both Young and Hering were correct. The brain uses primary colors, as determined by the cone opsins, to determine the wavelength of incoming light and hence its color. But the circuitry of the brain is complicated, and some of the cells in the brain that receive visual signals respond one way to one color and another way to its complement. Afterimages appear because cells adapt to, or become accustomed to, a certain situation if it endures for a while—just as the hearing system adapts to meaningless noise so that a person no longer hears or pays attention to it after a period of time. When the situation abruptly changes, as when the viewer shifts the gaze to a white object after staring at a colored one for so long, the brain is out of balance for a few seconds, and a ghost of the complementary color arises.

Color vision is best in the center of vision when the image is on the fovea, because there are few cone photoreceptors outside of the fovea. The periphery is for night vision, and a person cannot see color well at night or out of the corner of the eye. Experiments prove this: If a person stares straight ahead and a friend holds up a colored object to the side, the person cannot determine the color.

Some people have trouble with color all of the time. Estimates suggest that 5 to 8 percent of males are color-blind, although most of these individuals can see at least some color. Less than 1 percent of females are color-blind since the cause lies with genes found on the X chromosome—males have only one of this chromosome, but females have two, so they have a better chance of having at least one good copy of these genes. Dysfunctional copies of the genes result in cones that do not work or contain the wrong opsin. The most common type of color blindness is the inability to tell red from green, both of which may appear yellowish to affected individuals.

Eyesight: Problems and Solutions

Color blindness is not a serious disability in humans. Other visual problems, arising from an inability to focus, are far more serious. But unlike color blindness, there are solutions for most of these problems.

In the 1860s the Dutch ophthalmologist (eye doctor) Herman Snellen (1834–1908) devised the most common test for vision, based on the distance of 20 feet (6.1 m). The person being tested views a chart from a distance of 20 feet (6.1 m), and reads as many letters as possible. The letters decrease in size toward the bottom of the chart and depict the size that normally sighted individuals can read at various distances. The letters of the fourth row of the chart, for instance, are so large that most people can read them at 50 feet (15.2 m). But if a person standing 20 feet (6.1 m) away can just barely make them out, this person has 20/50 vision. Normal vision is 20/20, meaning the person can read the same-sized letters at 20 feet (6.1 m) that most people can.

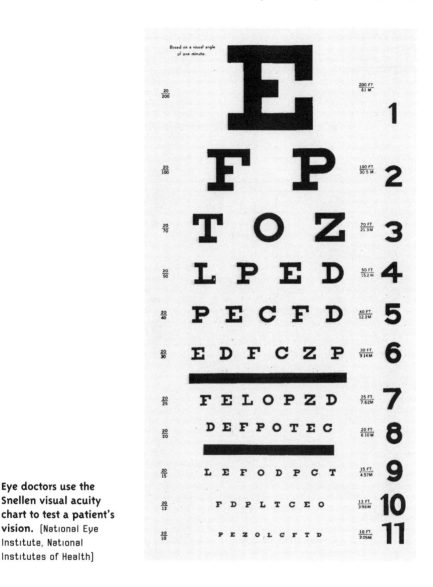

Eye doctors use the Snellen visual acuity chart to test a patient's vision. [National Eye Institute, National Institutes of Health]

This idea is still in use today, although eye charts are more complicated and are often shown on a viewing screen or monitor.

To focus an image well enough to read or see fine details requires proper refraction by the cornea and lens, and the retina must be located at the right spot. Even a small imperfection can lead to fuzzy vision.

The cornea is commonly at fault, either because it is not symmetric—which causes image distortion called *astigmatism*—or because it is not correctly curved. *Myopia*, or nearsightedness, is one of the most com-

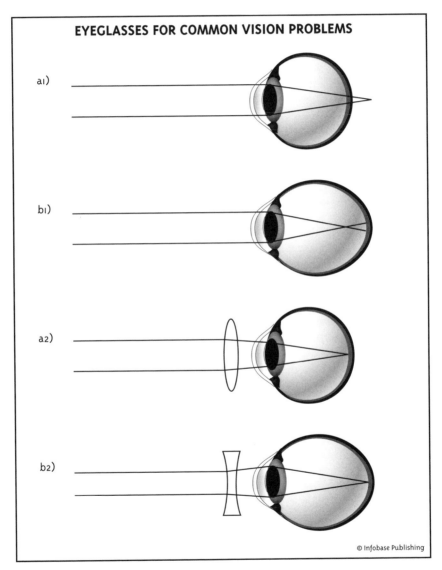

EYEGLASSES FOR COMMON VISION PROBLEMS

a₁)

b₁)

a₂)

b₂)

© Infobase Publishing

(a1) The eye of a farsighted person does not bend light enough to form an image on the retina. (a2) A convex lens helps farsightedness. (b1) The eye of a nearsighted person bends light too much. (b2) A concave lens helps nearsightedness.

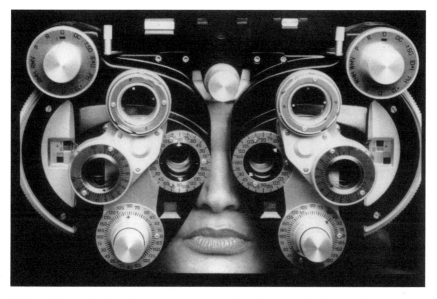

This machine, called a phoropter, measures refractive errors in the eye. [National Eye Institute, National Institutes of Health]

mon focusing problems, affecting about 25 percent of the population. A nearsighted person can focus on close objects but not those far away; the optics of the eye tend to form images in front of the retina instead of on it, as shown in part (b1) of the figure on page 64. By adjusting the lens, these people can focus on nearby objects, but the lens is not flexible enough to make corrections for distant objects. Part (b2) of the figure presents the solution: eyeglasses with concave lenses that cause divergence, spreading out the light rays by the correct amount so that the image forms on the retina instead of in front of it. The shape of the lens must be perfect, and since each person's eyes are slightly different, eyeglasses must be fitted to each person—one size does not fit all.

Hyperopia, or farsightedness, is the opposite problem, as seen in part (a1) of the figure. Many people are at least slightly farsighted—can see distant objects but have trouble focusing on nearby ones—and babies are generally always farsighted. In most people, the eye grows so that the farsightedness of their early years corrects itself and the eye forms the image on the retina instead of behind it. But some adults need eyeglasses with convex lens, as shown in part (a2) of the figure, to provide a little extra convergence. Farsightedness is also a common problem late in life; the lens of the eye becomes less flexible as a person ages, and it can no longer assume the shape it needs to focus on nearby objects. This problem, which will affect almost everyone at some point in their lifetime, is *presbyopia*. Older adults find they have to place a newspaper or book farther and farther away in order to read, until they finally need eyeglasses.

For nearsighted individuals, presbyopia presents a problem because they already need eyeglasses of a different kind. The solution to this dilemma, first developed by Benjamin Franklin, is bifocals—eyeglasses with two different types of lens glued together. The top half of the lens is usually for seeing distant objects and the bottom for nearby ones.

Brain and Vision

The optics of the eye—perhaps with a little help from eyeglasses—fixes the image on the retina. Photoreceptors convert the light into signals and pass the information on to the brain. Here, in the trillions of interconnected brain cells, is where people actually see the world.

Somehow the brain interprets what it sees based on experience (and some innate, or inborn, characteristics) and the environment. The *blind spot* shows one aspect of how the brain makes sense of the world. The blind spot exists because cells in the retina pass information to the brain using long, slender processes called axons, and these axons exit the eye at a certain point at the back. There are no photoreceptors at this spot, so a person cannot see there. People are not normally aware of the blind spot because it does not appear as a black, featureless region of the visual field—the brain fills in the spot with whatever surrounds it. Sometimes, what the brain fills in is incorrect, as can be seen by using the diagram in the following figure. By covering the left eye and staring at the cross with the right eye while slowly moving the picture back and forth, at some point the circle disappears. This happens when the circle is in the blind spot and the brain fills in the spot with what surrounds it—in this case, the white page.

Signals from the retina pass through several different areas of the brain. The physiologists David Hubel (1926–   ) and Torsten Wiesel (1924–   ) won the 1981 Nobel Prize in physiology for their work in recording the signals of cells in the visual system. By examining how cells respond to light and simple objects such as lines and contours, these scientists traced the information as it passed from cell to cell.

The most important part for seeing and interpreting complex pictures is the cerebral cortex, as mentioned in chapter 1. The cerebral

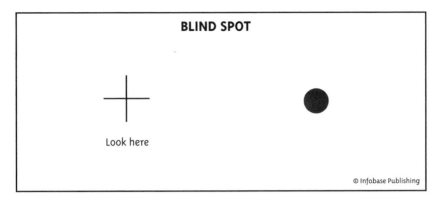

With the left eye covered, stare at the cross while slowly moving the book back and forth. At some range of distances, the circle disappears—it is in the eye's blind spot.

cortex is divided into many different areas, each devoted to a different purpose. One region of the cerebral cortex detects motion; people who suffer brain damage in this region have trouble seeing things that move. Another part of the cerebral cortex is primarily for color, and another part exists for piecing together the outline of objects. Scientists who study the brain do not understand how all of these parts come together to make the whole picture: People see a yellow car moving down the road, for example, even though each feature—the color, the object, and the motion—belongs to a different region of the brain.

People use the brain not just for seeing, of course, but also understanding—and an understanding of the subject of optics has led to an increased ability to see. Although people still do not fully know how the brain sees, the science of optics helped them to build instruments to see what the human visual system cannot. The following chapter examines two of the more important of these instruments: telescopes and microscopes.

TELESCOPES AND MICROSCOPES

The human eye and visual system are effective at gathering and focusing light and interpreting images, but there are limitations. To see the very small or the very distant, one needs to gather a great deal of light. A big eye would do the job: For example, animals that are active at night usually have large eyes in order to collect all available light. But for humans, the current size of the eye—about an inch (2.54 cm) in diameter—is sufficient to meet the most basic demands of finding food and avoiding predators, so there was no pressing need for anything larger to evolve.

This situation changed during the Renaissance. Medical advances and scientific observation required the means to examine small or distant objects well beyond the ability of the human eye and brain. To surpass the limitation of their visual systems, people developed optical instruments such as the microscope and telescope. The result opened up whole new worlds and the entire universe for exploration. The journey began in Holland.

Combining Basic Optics in Holland

Nobody is quite sure who invented the first compound microscope. As mentioned in chapter 2, pioneering opticians in the late Middle

Ages used single lenses as magnifying glasses, and the first spectacles appeared sometime in the 13th century. In the late 16th century, Holland had the most skilled lens-makers, and two of them—Hans Janssen and his son Zacharias—reportedly put two lenses together to make a compound microscope (a microscope with two or more lens). No written record exists of this first voyage in compound optics, and the exact date as well as actual identity of the discoverers is open to question. Given the expertise of Holland's craftsmen, though, it is likely that this country was the origin.

The use of two or more lenses made an instrument that was capable of much greater magnification than a single lens. Before the compound microscope, magnifying glasses had a power of perhaps 10x—they made objects look 10 times bigger—and some people called them flea glasses because these pests were a common object for which a person might search (and hope to destroy). Compound microscopes magnify objects up to 1,000 times or more, depending on how close the object is.

The telescope appeared at about the same time as compound microscopes were invented, and Holland and its excellent opticians were again the source. Dutchman Hans Lippershey noticed that an instrument made of a convex lens followed by a concave lens has the marvelous ability to bring distance objects closer. In 1608, Lippershey advertised the device, and word quickly spread. A year later, the famous Italian physicist Galileo Galilei made a telescope for himself and turned it toward the sky.

As illustrated in the following figure, the two lenses of compound instruments have different functions. The first lens is called the *objective lens*; in microscopes, the job of this lens is to bring the diverging rays of nearby objects and focus them to form an image. To do its job, an objective lens needs a lot of refractive power and is usually quite curved. The second lens, the eyepiece, magnifies this image. The total magnification of the microscope or telescope is the product of the magnification of all the lenses. Many of the telescopes used today have multiple lenses and split the light from the objective lens into two beams so that two eyepieces can be used, one for each eye.

The goal of an objective lens in a telescope is slightly different than in a microscope. Objects viewed in a telescope are distant and faint, so the objective lens needs to be large in order to gather as much light as possible. The same would be true of small objects viewed under a microscope except that, since they are at hand, shining bright light on them solves the problem.

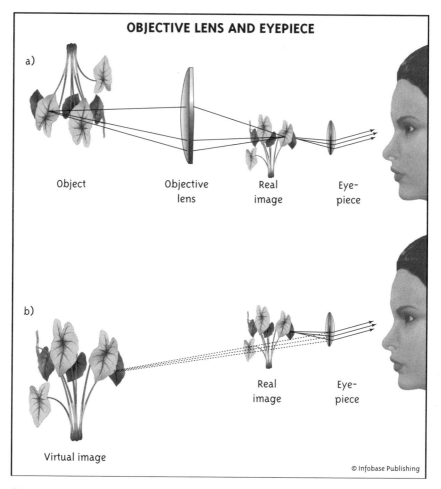

OBJECTIVE LENS AND EYEPIECE

a)

Object   Objective   Real   Eye-
                lens   image   piece

b)

                                Real   Eye-
                                image   piece

Virtual image

© Infobase Publishing

(a) The objective lens converges light from the object and forms a real image. (b) What the observer sees is a magnified virtual image created by the eyepiece.

A Magnified View

Microscopes revealed small environments—microcosms—that nobody had ever seen before. Magnifying glasses were a useful aid in the search and examination of tiny pests such as fleas, but people using these instruments already knew what they were looking for. With the magnifying power of hundreds of times, the early microscopes showed that life existed in unexpected places, such as a drop of water or a person's teeth.

Dutch scientist Antoni van Leeuwenhoek (1632–1723) was a particularly skilled maker and grinder of lenses. Leeuwenhoek was so careful and precise that even his simple (single-lens) microscope performed better than most of the compound microscopes of the 17th century. These powerful microscopes enabled him to see all kinds of strange and wonderful "animalcules," such as one-celled protists swimming around in a drop of pond water. Leeuwenhoek was also one of the first people to see bacteria; when he placed scrapings from his own teeth and those of other people under his microscope, he observed a large variety of tiny, living organisms. People of Holland in those days suffered terribly from tooth decay and other dental problems, though it would be many years before scientists understood the role of microorganisms. Leeuwenhoek reported his fascinating observations to the Royal Society, and the prestigious British scientific organization translated and printed these letters.

Another early microscopist was British physicist Robert Hooke (1635–1703). Hooke constructed some of the best compound microscopes of the 17th century and confirmed many of Leeuwenhoek's observations. Examining a thin slice of cork, Hooke discovered small, regular compartments that he called pores or cells—these compartments were the walls of plant cells that had been in the cork tissue. This discovery eventually led to the realization that all life consists of cells, either as single-celled microorganisms or many cells connected and working together, like most plants and animals, including humans.

People made fun of Hooke and Leeuwenhoek for studying what seemed to be insignificant, trivial objects. But scientists finally recognized the importance of these microorganisms, and the germ theory of disease eventually appeared. This was much needed because epidemics of smallpox, cholera, and other diseases killed millions of people and scientists had no explanation for these diseases. Then Frenchman Louis Pasteur (1822–95) and others argued that microorganisms or germs traveled by air or water and caused many of the diseases that have plagued humans throughout history. After accepting the germ theory of disease, people began taking these microorganisms seriously and learned how to avoid them. This development was the primary reason why life expectancy jumped from about 45 in the 19th century to 78 today.

But microscopes have their limits. Other diseases such as smallpox and polio did not seem to be caused by microorganisms because none showed up on microscope slides. Yet germs do cause these diseases—they are just too small for microscopes. The problem is that when light or any other wave encounters an obstacle or goes through an opening, the waves spread out—a phenomenon called *diffraction*. Diffraction blurs the image, and when the object is extremely small, it cannot be identified. The wavelength of a wave influences the amount of diffraction and its affects: Small wavelengths allow smaller objects to be seen before diffraction smears out the image. The ability to distinguish small objects is called resolution, and because light has such a small wavelength, the resolution of microscopes based on light is about 0.0000078 inches (200 nm).

Electron Microscopes

Although light microscopes can see many microorganisms, some of the smallest—viruses—average around 0.000004 inches (100 nm) in diameter, slightly below the resolution limit. Yet viruses are extremely important, not only causing annoying disorders such as colds but also deadly diseases such as AIDS and Ebola fever; even the flu, normally caused by less deadly strains of viruses, can become a serious hazard—40 million people died in the flu epidemic of 1918.

Reducing the resolution limit means finding a source of illumination with a smaller wavelength than light. The electromagnetic spectrum offers plenty of candidates—electromagnetic waves come in all wavelengths. But electromagnetic waves with small wavelengths, and therefore high frequencies, are not easy to handle and focus. A better option appeared in the 20th century when physicists realized that wave-particle duality applied to everything, not just light. In 1923 French physicist Louis de Broglie (1892–1987) found that a particle's wavelength λ is given by the equation

$$\lambda = \frac{h}{p},$$

where h is a small number called Planck's constant, and p is the particle's momentum. The momentum is the product of the particle's mass and velocity, and fast-moving electrons have very small wavelengths. Although nobody really understands how a particle like an electron can also behave as a wave, one of the greatest applications is "illumination" by electrons, the electron microscope.

In the early 1930s, physicists such as Ernst Ruska built the first electron microscopes. Because of the tiny "wavelengths" possible by electrons, electron microscopes can have resolutions as low as 0.000000004 inches (0.1 nm), and although most microscopes do not quite reach this limit, they are more than a thousand times more powerful than light microscopes. One of the earliest tasks for electron microscopes was to study viruses.

Electron microscopes are not without their difficulties. Light travels easily through air, but the relatively large molecules of air deflect tiny electrons, so the beams used in electron microscopes must be in a vacuum. Electron microscopes are bulky and expensive. But throughout the 20th century, electron microscopes were critical in the identification and study of viruses that wreak so much havoc on the world. Although today biologists have many tools to examine

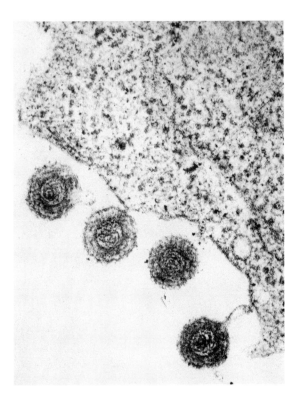

This is an electron microscope image of several particles of the human herpes virus-6. (Bernard Kramarsky, NCI Visuals)

viruses—such as instruments that detect and sequence viral genes—electron microscopes continue to be important in research on viruses as well as the smallest features of cells.

A Better View of the Universe

When people turned their lenses to the skies, they saw equally wonderful things. Galileo found many bodies that were invisible to the unaided eye, including four satellites of the planet Jupiter. Astronomy had been incorporated into religious teaching, and many prominent persons of the early 17th century were not pleased when Galileo used the telescope as part of his effort to overturn the belief that Earth was the center of the solar system. Earth, they thought, was special and therefore occupied the central position. Although officials tried to

This is a view looking down on the primary mirror of the northern Gemini 315.2-inch (8-m) telescope on Mauna Kea, Hawaii. (Gemini Observatory/NOAO/ AURA/NSF)

suppress the discoveries, Galileo and the scientists who followed him proved that the planets, including Earth, revolve around the Sun.

In order to inspect distant bodies, telescope must collect every possible ray of light. Like the eyes of nocturnal animals, telescopes should be large; often telescopes are specified by their diameters, such as the 200-inch (5-m) Hale telescope at the Palomar Observatory in California. But the use of glass for such large lenses is not possible; Hale and other large telescopes must use another optical surface—a mirror.

Small telescopes that use lenses are called refracting telescopes— the lens refracts the light rays to form an image. Refracting telescopes, used by Galileo and others (and still used today by many backyard astronomers), are useful, but since the objective lens is transparent, it must be mounted and supported on the sides. This becomes a problem if the lens is large because glass is heavy and tends to sag; although the distortion may not be much, focusing light requires a great deal of precision, and the delicate optical properties will be ruined. To keep a heavy object from sagging requires supporting the middle, but this would disrupt the light path.

Telescopes that use a mirror—reflecting telescopes—do not have this problem. As shown in the figure on page 76, a concave mirror focuses light to form an image. The rays are usually guided by a small secondary mirror to a location where the astronomer can view the image without blocking the light. The mirror can be large, such as the 200-inch (5-m) Hale reflector or the 315.2-inch (8-m) Gemini telescopes. Reflecting telescopes have an additional advantage: They do not suffer from chromatic aberration; this problem, as described in chapter 5, arises because glass refracts some wavelengths more than others and causes a blurry image. But a reflecting telescope suffers slightly from the secondary mirror and its weblike supporting rails being in the path of the light, which causes some interference. Both kinds of telescope also experience diffraction, though with large apertures, this is much less of a problem than with microscopes.

Large and carefully shaped mirrors have provided an amazing perspective on the universe. The Milky Way galaxy—the collection of stars and gas that includes the Sun and its planets—contains approximately 300 billion stars. In the 1920s, American astronomer Edwin Hubble (1889–1953) proved the faint clouds that early astronomers called nebulas are in many cases distant galaxies, each containing millions or billions of other stars. Planets outside the solar system are generally too small to be seen directly with telescopes, but as of September 2005, more than 150 extrasolar planets have been found by observation of

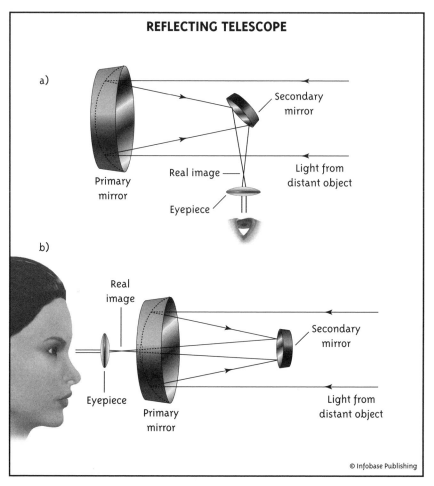

REFLECTING TELESCOPE

a)

Primary mirror

Secondary mirror

Real image

Light from distant object

Eyepiece

b)

Real image

Primary mirror

Secondary mirror

Eyepiece

Light from distant object

© Infobase Publishing

The mirror of a reflecting telescope focuses light, which is shunted either to the side, as in (a), or out a hole in the primary mirror, as in (b).

their gravitational effects on the stars around which they orbit. Telescopes have also shown that the universe is not static: Hubble and other scientists found that the universe is expanding.

Today's telescopes often have more than a single mirror. The Keck telescopes, located on Mauna Kea in Hawaii, have 36 mirrors that work together and function as if they were one 394-inch (10-m) mirror. Although having many parts to control can be a disadvantage, a single mirror of this size would be tremendously heavy and unwieldy. The Keck telescopes are some of the largest in the world.

Most of the large observatories are on remote mountaintops—Mauna Kea, for example, is 13,800 feet (4,200 m) high. The choice for location is inconvenient but necessary: No matter whether the telescope is refracting or reflecting or how many lenses or mirrors it has, the atmosphere is a problem. The distortion was noticed by Ptolemy all the way back in ancient times, as mentioned in chapter 2. To decrease the distortion caused by atmospheric refraction, astronomers position their telescopes as high as possible; the atmosphere decreases with altitude, and the thin air of mountaintops is cold and difficult to breathe, but it makes for much better observational conditions. Remote locations also decreases the stray light that masks faint objects—this can be seen by comparing the thousands of stars visible at night in the country with the hundreds, maybe only dozens of stars visible in large cities.

Space Telescopes

While mountaintops are better than sea level, there is still some air and atmospheric distortion. The ideal observatory is out in space—and so

The *Hubble Space Telescope,* shown orbiting against the background of the planet Earth [NASA]

the National Aeronautics and Space Administration (NASA) launched the *Hubble Space Telescope* in 1990. The *Hubble Space Telescope* orbits Earth at an altitude of about 375 miles (600 km), well above the atmosphere, and revolves around the planet once every 95 minutes. The primary mirror is seven feet (2.4 m) in diameter; although this is smaller than some of the larger ground-based telescopes, the *Hubble Space Telescope* produces fantastic images free from atmosphere distortion—and there is never a cloudy day in space. Astronomers use telecommunication to aim the telescope and retrieve the images.

But the vast potential of such a space telescope was almost lost because of a mistake in manufacturing the primary mirror. Although the error was tiny—the shape of the mirror was off by 1/50th of the diameter of a human hair—the small wavelengths of light mean optical instruments must be incredibly precise. As discussed in chapter 2, the proper shape of a mirror is a paraboloid, although spherical shapes are much easier to make; the term *spherical aberration* refers to a lack of focus in improperly shaped mirrors. The flawed telescope failed to focus some of the faintest objects, so a correction became necessary. In 1993, astronauts rode the space shuttle *Endeavour* into orbit and applied a fix consisting of a set of optical mirrors. Although some spherical aberration remained, further corrections in the processing of the images cleared up most of the rest of the problem.

Scientists have used the *Hubble Space Telescope* for many research projects: to study the expanding universe and measure the expansion rate; to show images of what are apparently massive black holes inhabiting the centers of many galaxies; to reveal the structure of the swirling clouds of gas and dust that will eventually become new stars and planetary systems; and to take many more breathtaking images of the universe. After 15 years, though, the telescope is nearing the end of its working life, and the *Hubble*'s ideal position in space—soaring above the atmosphere—also means that it is difficult to maintain. As of September 2005, NASA is unsure how much longer the *Hubble* will be maintained.

The loss of the *Hubble Space Telescope* will be a major blow to astronomy, but its replacement should also prove to be a productive instrument. NASA has scheduled the launch of the *James Webb Space Telescope* (*JWST*) in 2011, which will have 18 mirrors functioning as a 20-foot (6.5-m) device. The optics of the *JWST* is primarily intended for *infrared* light so that the telescope can better study the faint galaxies of the early universe—whose light is redshifted because of the expansion—but there will also be some function in the visible range as well.

This galaxy, imaged by NASA's *Hubble Space Telescope,* **is called the whirlpool galaxy.** (NASA/the Hubble Heritage team, STScI/AURA/N. Scoville, Caltech, and T. Rector, NOAO)

JWST will be much farther from Earth: about 1 million (1.6 km) miles away. Although budgetary problems may ultimately reduce the scope of the mission, astronomers eagerly await the launch.

Lenses and mirrors offered the earliest means for people to escape the confines of their world, even if only by examining the light from the very small and the very distant. Now that people have the ability to make electron microscopes and to put telescopes in space, even smaller and more remote worlds have become reachable. There has also long been a desire to make permanent records of images: to capture the light and permit everyone to get a good look. This is the job of optical electronics, discussed in the following chapter.

TAKING SNAPSHOTS OF THE WORLD: OPTICS AND ELECTRONICS

When the Soviet Union launched the first satellite, *Sputnik*, in 1957, the whole world suddenly came into view. Lenses and mirrors had been used since the Middle Ages to focus light and produce images, and the 19th century saw the development of cameras to record the images on photographic plates or film. The eye in the sky gave the science of optics a new vantage point, and people were quick to take advantage of it.

In early 1959, the United States tested the first photo reconnaissance satellite—part of a program called CORONA—and the satellite took its first image from space on August 18, 1960. An alternative term for such a satellite—spy satellite—specifies the goal of secretly taking pictures, and this was the mission of the series of CORONA satellites that operated from 1960 to 1972, taking 800,000 images. The U.S. government did not acknowledge the existence of these satellites until 1995, long after they were replaced by other, newer devices.

The early reconnaissance satellites faced a serious problem: In order to be useful, the film containing the images had to be brought

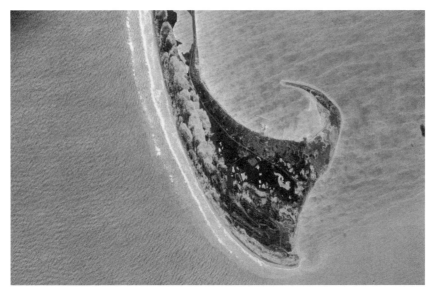

This photograph, snapped from the International Space Station, gives an aerial view of part of the Cape Cod National Seashore. [NASA]

down to Earth. This was done by ejecting the film in a capsule, with a parachute slowing the descent, and in many cases, the U.S. Air Force plucked these capsules out of the air with a midair retrieval. In the 1970s and 1980s, specially modified C-130 cargo planes flew over the Pacific Ocean, trailing grappling hooks and winches; the pilot flew directly over the parachute and hooked the fabric so that the crewmembers could haul it inside. This was a wild and dangerous business—and advances in optics and electronics eventually put these C-130s out of a job.

Charged-Coupled Devices

The *Hubble Space Telescope*, along with modern reconnaissance satellites, no longer has to record images on film and eject the capsules. Most imaging systems today use charge-coupled devices (CCDs).

A CCD consists of an array of electrical components that are sensitive to light and can store electrical charges. The absorption of light energy lifts atomic electrons into a higher orbit, and the absorption of a high-energy photon causes them to break away entirely—as in the photoelectric effect, discussed in chapter 4. Light striking the CCD liberates electrons, and the electrical components store these negatively charged particles as they accumulate. In short intervals of time, a circuit empties each little cell, or pixel, in the array, counting the number of electrons. The amount of charge is proportional to the amount of light striking the CCD, so the electrical circuit contains a signal that corresponds to the image that fell on the sensor surface. The signal is an electrical version of the image—an array of numbers representing the light from each pixel.

The resolution of a CCD depends on the number of pixels. A large number of pixels will produce a crisp image with a lot of details, and a small number of pixels results in a grainy image. This difference is similar to drawing with a sharpened, pointy pencil as opposed to one with a thick, bulky lead.

CCDs are perfect for reconnaissance satellites as well as the *Hubble Space Telescope.* The output of these devices is an electrical version of an image that can be easily transmitted down to the surface—no more midair retrievals of photographic film.

Even ground-based astronomers often choose CCDs over film, though of course for a different reason. The targets for all telescopes, whether on the ground or in orbit, are faint, so telescopes need all the light they can get. Their lenses or mirrors are accordingly huge, and CCDs help by making the most effective use of the output. CCDs are extremely efficient: Their electrical components capture about three-quarters of the light falling on them. Most photographic films manage to collect only a few percent of the light, so they require much more exposure to produce the same quality images. This makes CCDs enormously useful for optical instruments that must make the most of what little light is available, such as astronomical telescopes. CCDs are also used in scanners, which convert images and documents into computer files, and in filmless digital cameras.

Cameras

The first cameras preceded telescopes, though they did not have a lens. These primitive cameras, possibly used as far back as ancient Greece, were simply a box with a small hole. Pinhole cameras do not need a lens because only a few rays of light pass through the tiny hole, called an aperture, and the narrow passage "focuses" the light. The problem is that these few rays do not make a high-resolution picture, and if the image is to be recorded, it would take all day for enough light to get through to the film.

The solution is to use a lens. A lens can let a large amount of light inside the box but keeps the light focused by the glass's refractory properties. But where the image will form—how far behind the lens it will be—depends on the distance from the camera to the object whose image is being taken. The lens equation relates the focal length f of the lens to the object distance o and the distance i of the image from the lens:

$$\frac{1}{f} = \frac{1}{o} + \frac{1}{i}.$$

Chapter 5 defined the focal length as distance i of the image for a very distant object. The lens equation shows this is true, since for a large o, the term $1/o$ is nearly 0 and the equation reduces to $1/f = 1/i$, so $f = i$ in this case. In general, the closer an object is to the camera, the farther away the image is from the lens.

Focusing presents problems with cameras. Human lenses change shape, bending in order to refract the rays of close objects. The lenses of cameras are made of glass and are inflexible. As a result, cameras must move the lens or the film in order to focus on objects at different distances.

The depth of focus is also important. This is the range of distances that can be brought into focus; for a pinhole camera, almost all objects near and far can be focused, but for cameras with larger apertures—and the human eye—there is a smaller range. A wide aperture allows much light into the camera but also narrows the depth of focus, so in this case, the lens must be precisely positioned; in other words, the camera must be perfectly focused, or the image will be blurry.

Inexpensive cameras do not have many controls and are simply point-and-shoot devices. They are easy to use, but since they are not adjustable, these cameras provide clear pictures only under ideal con-ditions—motionless objects, located not too near the camera, under plenty of light. More expensive cameras have adjustable controls, let-ting the user choose the aperture and the amount of time that light is allowed to enter the camera (shutter speed). The user can decide if a wide aperture, which provides more light that may be needed for dark conditions, is important enough to override the concern over a narrower depth of focus. The shutter speed is critical for capturing fast-moving objects because if the film is exposed for a long time, the object will move during this period and will be blurred (if the object moves fast enough, its image will be nothing but a streak across the film). A fast shutter speed freezes the motion but requires better lighting because the film is not exposed for a long period of time. These tradeoffs are what make photography so interesting.

Camera lenses also vary from inexpensive and general purpose to costly and specialized. A serious problem is chromatic aberration, as discussed in chapter 5. All glass, including lenses, act somewhat like prisms in that they spread out the wavelengths (colors) of light. This means that not all wavelengths of light coming from an object will be focused properly, resulting in a blurry image. When a single piece of glass is used, there is little that can be done about this, so the solution is to make a lens by piecing together a number of different glasses. One type of glass may bend blue light more, another may bend red light more, and the combination, if precisely constructed, evens out the differences and all wavelengths (colors) come into focus. Expensive lenses may be composed of a dozen different elements to eliminate chromatic aberration.

Lenses also vary in their focal lengths. Wide-angle lenses have short focal lengths and project a large area onto the film, giving a wide, panoramic view. Telephoto lenses are the opposite: Their long focal lengths make a larger image but, of course, of a smaller area. Zoom lenses are complex devices with elements that make the focal length adjustable, allowing the photographer to choose the size of the image.

If reconnaissance satellites used a camera, they would need either a zoom lens to take pictures with different views or more likely a number of different cameras and lenses, each for different shots. But since satellites have such great altitude, they have the same problem as telescopes—to take pictures they need to gather as much light as possible. These eyes in the sky probably use a large mirror, as does the *Hubble Space Telescope*, except, of course, a reconnaissance satellite aims the mirror down toward the ground instead of up in the sky.

Most of the properties of today's reconnaissance satellites are secret—if people knew the resolution and location, they would be better able to hide. The current series of American reconnaissance satellites has been in use for three decades and goes by the name Keyhole. Estimates of the latest model are that it has a mirror larger than the one in the *Hubble Space Telescope* and can see objects on the ground as small as two inches (5 cm). But no one knows for sure.

Advances in optics and electronics mean better cameras as well as better reconnaissance satellites. Spying on the world has gone from

A Titan IV-B rocket takes off from Vandenberg Air Force Base in California on August 17, 2000, with the mission of placing a reconnaissance satellite into orbit. [USAF/Staff Sgt. Pamela Taubman]

awkward midair retrievals to a sophisticated telescopelike instrument that can probably read a license plate from space and beam the image back to Earth. No doubt reconnaissance satellites have proven useful in the conflicts with Iraq and the fight against terrorism, as well as monitoring the weaponry of belligerent nations. But some people wonder if these satellites might do more harm than good: Nobody likes to be spied upon, and a government that can watch a citizen's every step may be tempted to invade privacy. Like photography itself, there are tradeoffs involved in these issues, many of which are worth debating as optics and electronics continue to improve.

INVISIBLE ELECTROMAGNETIC RADIATION

Visible light forms only one small part of the broad electromagnetic spectrum. All of the waves (or photons) of this spectrum are electromagnetic, produced by electrical charges, and propagate at the same speed, the "speed of light"—186,200 miles per second (300,000 km/s) in a vacuum. All of the waves of the electromagnetic spectrum also travel in straight lines and interact with matter.

But electromagnetic radiation has an amazing variety and versatility. A patient with a broken bone gets an X-ray exam, a procedure that lets a physician examine the bone without opening the skin. Music and television broadcasters use radio waves to send programs to their audience, who might be miles away. *Microwave* ovens cook food. Rattlesnakes use infrared to see their prey in the dark. All of these types of electromagnetic radiation—X-rays, radio waves, microwaves, and infrared—differ only in frequency and wavelength.

Visible light has a frequency between 425 and 750 trillion hertz. This range of frequencies is abundant on the surface of Earth and human eyes evolved to respond to it, so visible light dominates the subject of optics and most of this book. Yet visible light is only a sliver of the whole, and this chapter describes a few of the many applications of the rest of the spectrum.

Radio Waves and Microwaves

When Hertz discovered radio waves in the 1880s, as discussed in chapter 3, he confirmed Maxwell's theory that electromagnetic waves exist—and that light is but a part of this broad spectrum. Radio waves are easy to produce and travel well in air, so broadcasters chose this portion of the electromagnetic spectrum. Radio transmissions came first, which is where the waves get their common name, but television broadcasters also use these waves.

Electromagnetic waves with a frequency below one gigahertz (a billion hertz) are called radio waves. The following equation relates the energy, E, of electromagnetic radiation to its frequency, f, and a number h, called Planck's constant:

$$E = hf.$$

The relation between frequency and energy makes sense in terms of the amount of effort required to produce a wave—high frequencies require more back and forth motion, so the wave has more energy. Low frequencies have little energy, and radio waves are the least energetic of the electromagnetic spectrum.

Although refraction and diffraction affects electromagnetic radiation, radio waves, like light, tends to travel in straight lines. This presents a difficulty for broadcasters since they need an unobstructed path to the radio or television receivers of their audience: Tall buildings and hills reflect radio waves and prevent clear reception by people in the "shadow" of the obstruction. To make their broadcasts available to the widest-possible region, broadcasters make their transmission from as great a height as they can. Antennae radiate the electromagnetic waves in all directions, and by placing the antenna at a high altitude, the transmission reaches a broad area. (The word *broadcast* refers to this broad area in which radio and television stations cast their radio waves.) For the same reason, recipients of the signals must also often raise their receiving antenna to obtain an unobstructed path.

In Philadelphia, Pennsylvania, for example, many of the local stations have antennae on a hill in the neighborhood of Roxborough, in

This news truck has raised its antenna in order to make a less obstructed path for the electromagnetic signals. [Kyle Kirkland]

the northwestern part of the city. More than a dozen towers of about 1,000 feet (305 m) in height dot the landscape, marking what some Philadelphians call the Roxborough tower farm.

Many natural sources of radio waves exist throughout the universe. The Sun, for instance, emits not only light but also radio waves and other parts of the spectrum. Astronomers study these waves with special telescopes called radio telescopes, similar to the optical instruments described in chapter 8. But since radio waves have such a low frequency—and consequently a long wavelength—radio telescopes behave a little differently. Chapter 8 of this book explained how resolution, the ability to "see" small objects, depends on the wavelength of the electromagnetic radiation; radio waves, with their long wavelengths, offer low resolution, so in order to distinguish more detail, radio telescopes must be quite large. The Arecibo telescope in Puerto Rico is 1,000 feet (305 m) in diameter, dwarfing optical telescopes.

Increasing the effective size of radio telescopes can be accomplished by linking different radio receivers together. In this way, individual elements, working together, can do the same work as a much bigger device that would be more difficult to build or operate. One of the largest radio observatories in the world is the Very Large Array, a network of 27 radio receivers, each 82 feet (25 m) in diameter, spread out in a Y-shaped configuration on a flat plain west of Socorro, New Mexico. The receivers are mobile, forming an array up to 22 miles (35 km) across. Astronomers combine the signals together to produce interference patterns; these patterns are like the bright and dark bands formed during Young's double-slit experiment but are more compli-cated. This radio observatory has been used to study many astronomi-cal objects, such as disks of dust and pebbles that will go on to form new planetary systems.

Microwaves are the next lowest frequency in the spectrum, occupy-ing the range from one to about 300 gigahertz. Astronomers also study microwave sources throughout the universe, but today these waves are probably best known for their use in microwave ovens. The use of microwaves to cook food suggests that they have a lot of energy,

Radio telescopes, part of the Very Large Array in New Mexico [Kyle Kirkland]

but this is false. Like radio waves, this low-frequency radiation is not particularly energetic. Microwaves cook food not because they deliver great quantities of energy but because they have the right frequency to swish water molecules back and forth, causing a significant amount of heat. Most foods have a lot of water, so microwaves raise their temperature while hardly affecting ceramic plates or plastic dishes.

Infrared and Ultraviolet

The electromagnetic waves most like visible light and closest in frequency are infrared and ultraviolet. Infrared has a slightly lower frequency (and longer wavelength) than the lowest frequency of light, which people perceive as red—so infrared gets its name from *infra*, meaning below, and *red*. Ultraviolet is on the other side of the spectrum, slightly higher (*ultra*) than the highest frequency of light, which is violet.

If human eyes were sensitive to infrared, the world would look much different because everything emits this form of radiation, including people. Warm objects emit more infrared than cooler ones because they have more energy, so people—with a skin temperature that is slightly less than the core body temperature of 98.2°F (37°C)—emit more infrared than an ice cube but less than asphalt on a sunny day. Hot objects such as the electrical element of a stove in operation have enough energy to emit a great deal of visible light, so a human eye can see its glow. But to a rattlesnake and other members of the pit viper family, everything glows—rattlesnakes have one pit on each side of the head filled with cells sensitive to infrared radiation. These sensors allow the snakes to hunt prey in the dark since animals are visible because of their body heat.

The surface of Earth absorbs a lot of sunlight during the day, raising the temperature and causing the emission of much infrared radiation. This radiation normally escapes into space, cooling the planet and allowing the temperature to drop during the night. But when something blocks this infrared from escaping—like the glass of a greenhouse—temperatures remain warm, even in the winter. The same thing may be happening on Earth on a global scale; people worry that gases such as carbon dioxide, methane, and others that block infrared will cause the surface temperature of Earth to rise. These gases are a common emission in the exhaust of factories and automobiles and have increased in conjunction with the rapid increase in industry of the last few centuries.

The slightly higher frequency and energy of ultraviolet is noticeable in that it can tan or burn human skin. The skin contains millions of cells that produce a brown pigment called melanin, though in different groups of people these cells produce differing amounts of melanin—little in fair-skinned people and much in dark-skinned people. Melanin offers protection from ultraviolet radiation (which has enough energy to damage cells) by absorbing the radiation and preventing it from striking cells. Exposure to light increases melanin production and darkens the skin. Most artificial lights emit little ultraviolet, but special lights used in tanning "beds" offer the prospect of a tan without the Sun.

X-rays and Gamma Rays

The highest-frequency, most energetic electromagnetic waves are X-rays and gamma rays. X-rays have a frequency between about 2.4×10^{16} and 5×10^{19} hertz, and any radiation beyond this is a gamma ray.

German physicist Wilhelm Röntgen (1845–1923) discovered X-rays in 1895, for which he received the first Nobel Prize in physics in 1901. People quickly recognized the medical applications of X-rays, and only a few months after the discovery of X-rays, this high-frequency radiation helped British physicians find a piece of metal accidentally buried in a woman's hand.

Since violent collisions produce high-energy radiation, X-ray machines generate X-rays by accelerating electrons and crashing them into large atoms. Small atoms such as hydrogen, oxygen, and carbon found in soft tissues of the body do not absorb many X-rays, but heavy atoms such as calcium and phosphorus found in bones absorbs a considerable number. X-rays pass relatively unimpeded through soft tissue—skin and organs—but bones block the high-frequency radiation, so they create a "shadow" on a film. In this way, the image of bones (or pieces of metal lodged in the body) show up on X-ray films, giving physicians a view into the body without surgical incision.

Whereas low-energy microwaves work together to produce heat by churning water molecules, single X-ray photons have enough energy to break apart molecules. Tearing loosely held electrons from metal, as in the photoelectric effect discussed in chapter 5, does not require a great deal of energy, but ripping a tightly bound electron from an atom or breaking chemical bonds does. Powerful radiation such as X-rays and gamma rays are known as ionizing radiation for their ability to create ions—particles that have been charged by the loss or gain of charges such as electrons. Ionizing radiation damages the cells of an organism, especially long, vulnerable molecules such as deoxyribonucleic acid (DNA). Severe damage to DNA kills cells. Medical uses of X-rays are careful to deliver a minimum amount of radiation, sufficient to provide an image but not enough to injure tissue.

Ionizing radiation is one of the hazards of nuclear explosions, but in certain circumstances, it can be beneficial. Cancer is the second-leading cause of death in America and occurs when a cell or cells of the body begin to grow and divide uncontrollably, forming tumors or other abnormal tissue that invades healthy tissue. Cells that frequently divide are especially susceptible to the damage caused by ionizing radiation, so radiation therapy by gamma rays or X-rays is a common form of treatment for these diseases. Physicians try to concentrate the radiation on the cancerous cells, but some healthy tissue almost always becomes unintentionally affected; these side effects tend to occur in rapidly growing tissue such as skin, hair, and intestine—causing burns, hair loss, and nausea—but the most important thing is that the treatment is frequently successful if the cancer is caught early.

Like all the other forms of electromagnetic radiation, the universe contains many sources of X-rays and gamma rays. One of the most interesting of these sources is a black hole, in which a large mass has become so condensed that it creates an area of ultrahigh gravity. As bits of matter such as dust particles floating in space fall toward the black hole, they accelerate, heat up, and emit X-rays. Astronomers study black holes by studying the X-ray emissions, although there is a problem: Earth's atmosphere prevents most X-rays from reaching the ground. From a health standpoint, this is excellent, but for astronomers, this means that they must rise above the atmosphere in order to study astronomical X-ray sources.

One of the most important X-ray observatories is the *Chandra* satellite, launched in July 1999. An X-ray observatory differs from radio or light telescopes because of the energy of this radiation; X-rays are difficult to focus and do not harmlessly bounce off mirrors but are energetic enough to burrow into them. In order to guide and concentrate X-rays, the mirrors of *Chandra* are configured so that the radiation grazes them at a large angle, ricocheting instead of being absorbed. The mirrors are nearly parallel to the X-rays, and *Chandra*'s X-ray telescope has an odd appearance resembling a barrel.

Human eyes tune into visible light, which is among the brightest of the Sun's radiation to get through the atmosphere, but this small range is only a fraction of the electromagnetic spectrum. Other frequen-

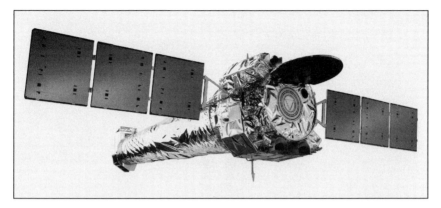

Astronomers use the *Chandra X-ray Observatory,* launched by the space shuttle *Columbia* on July 23, 1999, to study distant X-ray sources throughout the universe. The observatory was named after the Indian-American astrophysicist Subrahmanyan Chandrasekhar, who won the 1983 Nobel Prize in physics for his study of the structure and evolution of stars. [NASA/CXC/SAO]

cies and wavelengths present abundant opportunities for nonoptical but important and fascinating applications. Another important use of electromagnetic radiation demands a precise control over the wave's frequency and wavelength, as well as its phase. Devices that accomplish this are lasers, the subject of the following chapter.

11

LASERS

For a given unit of area, lasers are much brighter than the Sun, and science fiction movies portray them as efficient weapons of light. But the usefulness of lasers lies not so much in their power as in their narrow, *coherent* beams of a single wavelength.

Light from the Sun or from most lamps comes in all different frequencies jumbled together. Even waves of the same frequency may have different phases—one may be cresting while the other is in a trough. Light from a laser is distinct, though it does share some properties with ordinary kind of light: Laser beams travel at the same speed, and they have the same electromagnetic nature. But laser light has coherency—the waves have the same wavelength and travel in-step, locked together in the same phase as if they were a single wave.

Coherent light produces tight beams, as seen in the futuristic movies and television shows when "ray guns" are fired. But lasers in real life have yet to catch up to this kind of application and probably never will; real lasers must obey the laws of physics, unlike movie lasers. The energy of a laser beam maintains the same relation as ordinary light—based on frequency and not amplitude—and physics has played a critical role in lasers from their very beginning, in the 1920s, when Albert Einstein worked on the theoretical concept of stimulated emission.

Stimulated Emission

The word *laser* is an acronym for light amplification by stimulated emission of radiation. Spontaneous emission occurs when atoms and electrical charges emit random bursts of light. Stimulated emission is the process by which a single photon stimulates the emission of identical photons, building up a coherent beam of light, the laser.

A laser generally has three components: a source to pump energy into the system, a medium in which stimulated emission occurs, and a pair of mirrors that bounce photons back and forth across the medium. Lasers are often named for the medium; the first laser, built in 1960 by Theodore H. Maiman at Hughes Research Laboratory in California, was a ruby laser—the medium was a small ruby.

Stimulated emission requires a medium that can maintain a large number of atoms in an excited state, meaning they have enough energy to emit a photon. Most of the atoms of a substance are normally in an unexcited, or ground, state, so lasers need a population of atoms that are in the opposite, or inverted, state; this is called a population inversion.

The job of the energy source is to provide the excitation. In many lasers, the energy comes from a bright (ordinary) light shined on the medium or from electrical discharges. When the population inversion occurs, the medium is ready, but not just any medium is effective because if the atoms simply emit their energy in the form of random bursts of light—spontaneous emission—the laser will not work. In order to make a useful laser, a medium must have a relatively stable excited state so that atoms can stay there, waiting to be stimulated. Many different types of media are possible, and each gives the laser certain characteristics, as described in the following section.

As illustrated in the figure on page 96, energetic atoms in the medium emit photons, and soon one of these, by chance, takes a path that leads it to bounce from one mirror to the other, through the medium. The photon has the right energy to stimulate other atoms (the photon came from one of the atoms in the first place), and as the photon passes through the medium, it stimulates the emission of other, identical photons. This stimulated emission results in an amplification of the initial photon, which is how lasers get their name. The photons bounce between the mirrors and multiply until they reach a magnitude large enough to seep through one of the mirrors—one of the pair is

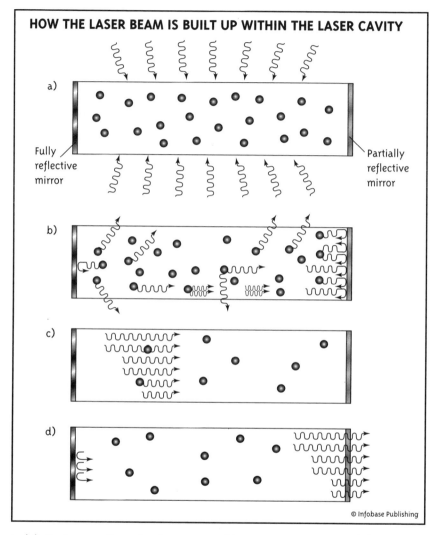

HOW THE LASER BEAM IS BUILT UP WITHIN THE LASER CAVITY

In (a), the laser medium absorbs energy and begins emitting photons (b). After stimulated emission, the photons form a coherent wave, as in (c), and exit upon reaching high intensity (d).

usually not fully reflective but allows some light to pass through at high intensities so the laser beam can exit the device.

The identical photons are coherent. The operation is similar to a group of people shouting the same chant in unison, producing loud but understandable words—a much different result than the murmuring of a group of people spontaneously talking among themselves, speaking at random times and saying different things. Laser light differs from spontaneously emitted light in intensity (laser beams are naturally bright), directionality (the light has a specific direction), monochromaticity (lasers emit a single wavelength, or color), and coherence (in-phase).

The Spectrum of Lasers

All lasers have the same basic operation, but they do not generate the same type of beam. The spectrum of lasers is as varied and colorful as the spectrum of electromagnetic radiation.

The frequency and wavelength of the laser beam depends on the energy states of the medium's atoms. Since the medium is so important in determining the properties of a laser, lasers usually carry the name of the medium (such as the ruby laser). Lasers may also be described by the frequency of their emission: infrared, ultraviolet, X-ray, and others. The earliest device to use stimulated emission was known as a *maser*—microwave amplification by stimulated emission of radiation, developed a few years before the laser—and many people still call a laser that emits microwaves or radio waves by this term.

A ruby laser—the first laser to be built—produces visible light of a long wavelength in the red portion of the spectrum. This laser was more difficult to build than the earlier maser because light has more energy (higher frequency and shorter wavelength) than microwaves or radio waves, which means the laser is harder to pump. The laser built by Maiman was only about an inch (2.54 cm) long and less than 0.33 inches (0.85 cm) in diameter and was not capable of much power.

Ruby lasers use a solid medium, but helium-neon is another common type of laser that uses a mixture of gases as its medium. Helium-neon lasers also produce light in the red portion of the spectrum but at a slightly smaller wavelength than ruby lasers. Many other lasers produce beams with wavelengths in the infrared or ultraviolet range (these devices are almost always called lasers although their output is not visible light). The carbon dioxide (CO_2) laser has a gaseous medium and was one of the earliest lasers to be built, shortly after the ruby laser, but its wavelength is in the infrared portion of the electromagnetic spectrum. Lasers made of semiconductor diodes—small electrical components that conduct currents under certain conditions—also generate infrared beams. Excimer lasers use a mixture of gases such as xenon, chlorine, or fluorine that form excited combinations (dimers) of molecules as the medium; the output of these lasers is ultraviolet radiation.

X-ray lasers would have an extremely energetic beam, but for that reason, they are difficult to build and require enormous power sources. Devices tested in the 1980s by the U.S. military had as their source a nuclear explosion—an event capable of releasing vast amounts of energy but also an event full of hazards and not exactly convenient for the operation of a laser.

But laser beams can be continuous, or they can be pulsed, consisting of brief pulses of radiation that do not require as much energy. The Lawrence Livermore National Laboratory in California constructed a laser that creates a brief X-ray beam lasting only a billionth of a second from an exceptionally high-energy light pulse. Still, the heat is so severe that this laser can be fired only a few times a day or it will overheat. Smaller X-ray lasers at Livermore work on less energy and require only a few minutes to cool down. Even more practical devices are possible with energy from particle accelerators—large machines designed to create and accelerate small particles—such as the Los Alamos Advanced Free-Electron Laser in New Mexico.

Lasers in Civilian Life

An X-ray laser is obviously not the right tool for every job. But with the right combination of power and wavelength, lasers of all different types serve a variety of roles in everyday life.

The helium-neon laser mentioned earlier is a common laser, and the red light from these low-power devices provides excellent laboratory demonstrations. These lasers are also often used in bar-code scanners at the supermarket and other stores, a process that reduces checkout time so that consumers do not have to wait in long cashier lines. All packages or containers now display a bar code—a series of bars that identify the product. Laser beams illuminate the bar codes, which are read by a scanner. The machine then retrieves the price of the item from the store's computer.

Semiconductor lasers, also called diode lasers, are so small that a person can hold dozens in the palm of one hand. They are one of the most common lasers, and nearly everyone uses them since compact disc (CD) and DVD players contain one. CDs and DVDs store music, movies, or data in a digital format, with long strings of digits coding the information in a binary language. The digits can be either a 1 or a 0, and words formed from these digits stand for certain quantities or letters; for instance, 1000001 represents the letter *A* in text code. A huge number of digits can be stored on the discs as tiny bumps or pits, which in DVDs can be as small as 0.000016 inches (0.4 µm) long. These pits form a narrow, spiraling track around the DVD that if stretched out would have a length of 7.5 miles (12 km). The pits or bumps change the reflective properties of the disc, but reading these tiny hills requires a concentrated source of light, a laser.

Excimer lasers find widespread use in surgery. Their tight beams allow precision, and the ultraviolet radiation is sufficiently powerful to cut, burn, or sculpt tissue. Chapter 17 discusses these procedures.

Lasers are also excellent in surveying tasks. Finding the distance between any two points is easy because the speed of light is known, and surveyors need only measure the time required for a pulse of light to travel the whole length. Any light source would do, but lasers do not spread out much, so a low-power beam can travel large distances and still be detectable.

Perhaps the ultimate surveying task was to measure the distance between Earth and the Moon, which scientists accomplished with lasers after Apollo astronauts brought special reflectors to the surface of the Moon. A narrow beam from an argon gas laser on Earth made the 280,000-mile (400,000-km) trip and spread out only to a diameter of a couple of miles, tight enough so the reflection of the Moon could be detected back on Earth. Such a measurement would not be possible without lasers because even the most powerful light source would spread out so widely that it would not be measurable over such distances. Lasers allowed the measurement of the Earth-Moon distance to within four inches (10 cm).

One of the most important uses of lasers is still in the development stage but if successful would bring about a cheap, safe, and abundant source of energy. Fusion, the process that powers the Sun and other stars, occurs when the nuclei of small atoms combine to form a larger nucleus; in the process, a great deal of energy is released. Although fusion bombs have already been made, a fusion power plant is not yet practical—the necessary conditions mimic the interior of the Sun, millions of degrees in temperature and high pressures. But training high-power laser beams on a small target can briefly reproduce such an extreme environment, allowing fusion to take place on Earth in a controllable manner.

The 10-story-high National Ignition Facility (NIF) building is as big as a football stadium. When completed, it will house a 192-beam laser system. [University of California/Lawrence Livermore National Laboratory/Department of Energy]

This illustration shows an aerial view of the NIF, with a computer-aided graphic drawing of the internal components. On the left end of the building are the optical devices and lasers, the beams of which are routed toward the right end, which houses the target chamber. [University of California/Lawrence Livermore National Laboratory/Department of Energy]

The Lawrence Livermore National Laboratory is presently building the world's largest laser system, called the National Ignition Facility (NIF), in order to accomplish controlled fusion, among a number of other goals. When completed in the next few years, the NIF will have 192 high-power lasers capable of briefly exceeding the annual electrical power output of the entire nation. The building to house the lasers, located in Livermore, California, and finished in September 2001, spans 600 feet (183 m)—two football fields in length.

Ray Guns and Star Wars

Lasers are classified in categories from I to IV, with IV being the most powerful and dangerous. The lasers of the NIF obviously have to be used with care, but all lasers require safety precautions, particularly those with invisible beams that can damage an eye before the person is even aware of it.

A concentration of electromagnetic energy like a laser beam—or a focused beam of sunlight from a lens or mirror—will heat whatever it strikes. This was the goal of the burning mirrors Archimedes may or may not have constructed, and science fiction writers have suffered no lack of futuristic weapons when it comes to lasers. Yet the physics of these devices prescribes some constraints—not always followed in fiction and movies—and even though lasers have been around for 45 years, "ray guns" are not commonplace.

Handheld lasers with enough energy to destroy targets are not a likely prospect. Beams cause damage from their intensity or high-frequency (and therefore high-energy) or both. But powerful lasers require huge energy sources, as the previous sections indicate, so unless some as yet unknown, compact source can be found, a deadly weapon that emits continuous waves or lengthy pulses is not going to fit into anyone's palm.

Lasers are also not effective weapons on a large scale. The destruction of a city or even a large building is not likely because the energy of a laser concentrates into a tight beam, incapable of affecting a broad area. The nature of lasers is to make a coherent beam of light, and effective weapon systems must take advantage of this property. The concentrated energy of laser light is ideal to heat and destroy a small, moving target, and this was the primary goal of the U.S. military's Strategic Defense Initiative (SDI), described by then President Ronald Reagan in 1983.

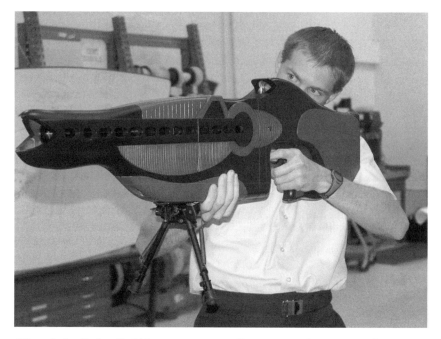

Although deadly handheld lasers are not a reality yet, Captain Drew Goettler demonstrates the Personnel Halting and Stimulation Response, or PHaSR. The PHaSR is a portable, nonlethal deterrent that flashes a laser light intended to dazzle and temporarily blind rioters or aggressors. [USAF]

In the 1980s, the cold war between the United States and the Soviet Union had been going on since the end of World War II in 1945, and both countries had amassed huge stockpiles of nuclear missiles capable of obliterating the entire world. SDI's mission was to protect the United States against a missile attack by destroying incoming missiles before they reached their target. The instruments needed to accomplish this formidable proposal were tracking satellites to detect rocket launches and orbiting X-ray lasers to strike and destroy the missile. Much of this technology had not yet been developed, and critics called the proposal Star Wars, linking it to far-in-the-future science fiction.

The U.S. government spent $40 billion in the 1980s and 1990s on the project. Despite the development of some new and better lasers, nothing approaching the original vision of SDI was ever realized. But the collapse of the Soviet Union in the early 1990s changed the balance of power, and the United States was no longer facing a bombardment by thousands of missiles. Today the most serious threat to the country's security comes from terrorism or from small nations or dictators that may gain control of a nuclear missile. Stopping one or just a few missiles is a much more feasible task, and a small-scale version of SDI may soon exist. Instead of X-ray lasers in satellites, there will be an airborne laser system, housed in a modified Boeing 747, flying at about 40,000 feet (12,200 m). The current design for the high-power laser has a chemical oxygen iodine medium; a reaction between the chemicals in the medium produces energy, and excited iodine atoms generate an intense infrared beam. This laser would be able to overheat and destroy a missile from a distance of hundreds of miles. The system is being tested and may become operational as soon as 2008.

Another laser weapon is the Tactical High-Energy Laser (THEL), which uses a deuterium fluoride chemical laser to destroy small rockets or artillery shells. In a 2004 test, the laser destroyed incoming mortar shells, showing that it could protect troops in the battlefield. The U.S. military might use these defensive systems in the near future.

Laser applications span a wide range of activities, as varied as lasers themselves. From the home to the battlefield, these devices perform valuable services. There is yet another widespread use of lasers and, though unseen, plays a critical role in letting people—and computers—talk to one another. The use of light in communication is the subject of the following chapter on fiber optics.

FIBER OPTICS AND OPTICAL COMMUNICATION

In 1885, Geronimo broke out of a reservation and, with dozens of his fellow Apache, led the U.S. Army on a long chase through the territory of Arizona. Army troops searching for the defiant Apache needed to communicate with one another, but radio had not yet been invented, so the army turned to sunlight: They used a heliograph, an instrument consisting of a mirror or mirrors to reflect the Sun's rays and flash messages in Morse code to a distant location. With heliograph stations on hills or mountaintops throughout the region, the army could relay messages across 800 miles (1,280 km) in a few hours.

General Nelson Miles and his troops finally cornered Geronimo's band in 1886, and although the heliograph played a role in this effort, the instrument was not widely used in many other campaigns. The heliograph system worked for General Miles and his troops because the stations were visible for long distances and because the communication medium—sunlight—was abundant in Arizona. These conditions do not always exist elsewhere.

Searchlight beams have also been used for Morse code messages between ships at sea, particularly navy vessels that must maintain radio silence for tactical reasons. Light as a communication medium has its advantages—it is easy and cheap—but the dots and dashes of

Morse code, represented by flashes of light, are cumbersome. Another problem is that light travels in a straight line, so it cannot follow the curvature of Earth; the heliograph stations of General Miles needed to have one another in sight, limiting the distance by which they could be separated. What is needed is a way to get light to follow any sort of path whatsoever, the same way that electricity flows down copper wires. This is exactly what fiber optics does, and in the 1970s, this technology opened up a new era in optical communication.

A New Means for Guiding Light

Chapter 5 discussed refraction—the bending of light as it passes from one material to another. When light travels from a material with a high index of refraction, such as glass, to a material with a low index of refraction, like air, the ray bends away from the normal (if it strikes the interface between the two materials at an angle). The interface always reflects a portion of the light, but when the rays strike at a shallow angle, transmission does not occur, and all of the light reflects away from the boundary. Part (a) of the following figure illustrates refraction at various angles. *Total internal reflection* occurs when light barely grazes the interface and all the rays are reflected.

Total internal reflection is actually a kind of refraction. As the figure shows, rays striking the interface at increasingly shallow angles travel more closely to the interface itself. Finally, at the critical angle, the ray is bent all the way back onto itself, so no light passes through the interface—total internal reflection. This happens only when the second material has a lower index of refraction than the first. The value of the critical angle depends on the two materials; for a light ray passing from glass with an index of refraction of 1.5 to air, which has an index of refraction of 1.0003, the critical angle as measured from the normal is about 42 degrees.

Fiber-optic cable takes advantage of total internal reflection by trapping the light inside a thin cylinder of glass or plastic, as shown in part (b) of the following figure. Even though the cylinder may be bent, light always grazes the interface, and so it never gets beyond the critical angle.

Another device to channel light could be built with a tube that has a shiny, mirrorlike inside surface, and light beams would be reflected along the inside of the tube. But such a device would not work nearly as well as a fiber-optic cable. One of the advantages of an optical fiber is

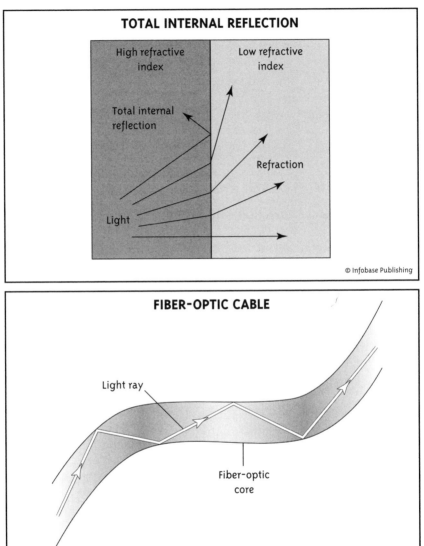

(a) Light rays can pass from a material with high refractive index to a material with a low refractive index until the angle becomes too great—then all rays reflect. (b) Because of total internal reflection, the light rays of a fiber-optic cable do not pass through the boundary, even though it is transparent.

its flexibility—a mirrored tube would be rigid. Another problem with mirrors is that they not only reflect light, but they also absorb it, and a light signal sent down a "light pipe" would soon diminish to nothing.

The core of an optical fiber is made of a finely drawn glass of about 0.0004 inches (10 µm) in diameter. Surrounding the core is the cladding—a thicker material with a decreased index of refraction so that light will bounce off the interface. A strong plastic coating covers the core and cladding, protecting them from damage, and the whole fiber has a diameter of about 0.005 inches (125 µm). A fiber-optic cable may contain hundreds or even thousands of optical fibers bundled together.

Since light travels through the core, this glass must be extraordinarily transparent if the optical fiber is to be of a useful length. One of the difficulties of early versions of fiber-optic technology was making glass with a suitable transparency. Even a windowpane of less than an inch (2.54 cm) in thickness stops a portion of light, and a fiber must be exceptionally clear if it is to carry an optical signal across a distance of miles. Impurities decrease a glass's transparency, so optical fibers are made only from the purest of materials. In 1970, Robert Maurer, Donald Keck, and Peter Schultz, working at a company called Corning, developed a glass fiber that would not lose most of its light for a length of about a half mile (0.8 km). The fibers of today can sustain a signal for more than 100 times this length. If the oceans were as transparent as this glass, even the deepest trench could be seen.

Communicating with Lasers and Hair-Thin Glass

Fiber optics would not be useful without sources of coherent light—lasers, the subject of the previous chapter. But the advantages of optical communication have more to do with frequency.

A message requires variability—some sort of changing signal. A constant tone of 500 hertz is boring and could carry little information, and a book containing the letter *A* repeated thousands of times would also be useless. Radio waves carry information broadcast by television or radio stations by varying some part of the signal, either amplitude or frequency or phase of the wave. The amount of information a wave can carry depends on how much it can change, and light, with its higher frequency, has a capacity several thousand times higher than radio waves.

Lasers are effective communication tools because their light does not spread out much. As mentioned in the previous chapter, laser beams have traveled from Earth to the Moon and back and maintained enough strength to be detectable. But lasers suffer from one of the same limiting factors as the heliographs of General Miles and his troops—the need for senders and receivers to be in one another's line of sight. The optical fibers and total internal reflection eliminate this factor, and the laser provides a light intense enough to be used in these tiny cylinders of glass or plastic. The combination of hair-thin fibers and lasers is what makes fiber optic communication work.

Until the last few decades, most telephone conversations have been carried by copper wires, but fiber optics enjoys numerous advantages. Light has a high information carrying capacity, and because optical fibers are so thin, more of them can be packed into a cable than copper wires. Light-carrying fibers do not interfere with one another, unlike current-carrying wires that generate electromagnetic fields and disrupt the signals of other wires in the vicinity. These fields also allow people to listen in on conversations without even breaking the connection, making wire a less secure medium of communication than optical fibers.

Fiber-optic systems contain several components: transmitters to generate the light and encode the information, fibers to carry the transmission, repeaters to prevent the light from fading over long distances, and receivers to decode the signals and transform the information into another form, such as speech or video. Repeaters are often necessary because optical fibers may stretch for lengths beyond their capability to transmit light. In these cases, the light would diminish and be lost except for periodically spaced repeaters to boost the weakened signal.

To squeeze the most advantages out of fiber optics, these systems generally use infrared radiation rather than light. The reason is that glass is more transparent to wavelengths in the infrared portion of the spectrum than visible light; since this means that optical fibers can be longer without the need for repeaters, infrared performance is superior.

Semiconductor lasers are ideal for fiber-optic systems. They are small, emit a lot of light, have a long life, and can be switched on and off at a high rate, allowing the information to be encoded. Semiconductor lasers are so tiny that they can often be packaged along with the optical fibers, which means that the people installing the cables do not have to align or configure the whole system.

In the earliest fiber-optic networks, repeaters were bulky signal detectors and regenerators and were expensive to incorporate into the system. Although glass transparency has improved, networks today

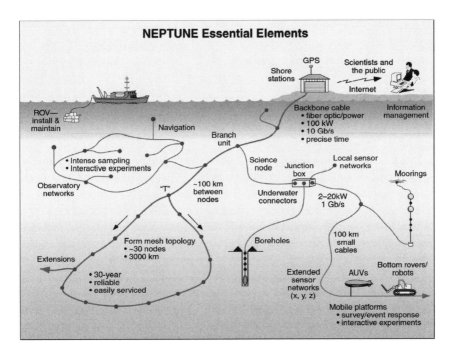

NEPTUNE is a joint U.S./Canadian project, with the U.S. program office located at the University of Washington in Seattle. The project will provide a network of sensors, linked by fiber optics, around a large area in the northeastern Pacific Ocean, just off the northwest coast of the United States and southwest Canada. The network will allow scientists and students to monitor oceanic events such as submarine volcanic eruptions. Portions of NEPTUNE are scheduled to begin operations in 2007. [NEPTUNE Project/Paul Zibton]

continue to require repeaters, and many systems use optical amplifiers, consisting of a special section of fiber excited by a laser. The weakening signal stimulates emission of light and is amplified, like the amplification of a photon in a laser medium. With periodic boosts, signals in fiber-optic networks can travel all the way around the globe.

The Modern World of Communication

Fiber optics carries a considerable portion of the information transmitted by today's telecommunication networks. A large number of local and long-distance telephone calls, cable television transmissions, and links between computers work through optical fibers. Yet fiber optics has not completely replaced radio waves or copper wires since fiber-optic systems require an expensive initial investment—the cables, transmitters, and receivers must be bought and installed—and unlike electricity in copper wires, light does not offer a convenient way to power remote devices in the way that, for instance, a telephone draws its power from the phone lines.

Still, the advantages outweigh the disadvantages for many large-scale projects. In the late 1970s and early 1980s, telephone and network companies such as AT&T and GTE (now Verizon) began installing fiber optics. Television quickly followed, and fiber optics carried some of the video during the coverage of the winter Olympic Games at Lake Placid, New York, in 1980. The first transatlantic fiber-optic cable appeared in 1988 (this was the eighth transatlantic cable, the prior lines being wire), with repeaters averaging 30–40 miles (48–64 km) apart. The expense of building and installing the cable was over $350 million, but due to its high information capacity, the fiber-optic cable reduced the cost per circuit by a factor of 100.

The slow link in the chain of modern communication systems is the copper wire in houses and small businesses. Most individuals cannot afford to buy fiber-optic systems, so when they make a telephone call from home over a "land line," their voice must make at least a portion of its journey over old-fashioned wire—noisy, slow, but generally reliable. This is also true for some of the connections made by home computers to the colossal network of computers known as the Internet.

Large "backbones" of the Internet consist of high-speed fiber-optic cables, and a huge amount of text, graphics, and video constantly travel up and down these lines; every second, the cables transmit an amount of information equivalent to many books. But many Internet users in homes and small businesses connect their computer to the Internet by linking with computers of a company through relatively slow telephone wires. The computers of these companies, called Internet service providers, make connections with the high-speed lines of the Internet.

The Internet provides e-mail and Web sites by which a growing fraction of communication and business transactions are conducted, and fiber-optic networks offer the necessary speed and information capacity. Wires and wireless devices such as cell phones, wireless networks, and broadcast stations are important components of modern communication systems, but light—or the infrared portion of the spectrum—carries a considerable portion of the traffic, whether it is over the Internet or the telephone. Light will continue to replace electrons and wires in future communication networks. And as the following chapter shows, light may also do the same in another common and essential instrument, the computer.

OPTICAL COMPUTING

The word *computer* once referred to a person who excelled in performing calculations quickly and accurately. The early calculating machines were bulky mechanical contraptions full of gears and levers, slow and time-consuming to operate, and people were generally more reliable. In the 1940s, faster electronic computers became available, such as ENIAC—Electronic Numerical Integrator and Calculator—developed by engineers John Eckert and John Mauchly in 1946. But electronics also has limitations, and future computers may be based instead on photonics—photons of light rather than electrons and electrical currents.

Light is fast and less susceptible than electrons to interference and resistance. Resistance of wires and circuits to the flow of electrons is particularly important because it causes heating, which tends to destroy delicate electrical components. Light travels through air or the glass of an optical fiber with little resistance. Optical computers offer the potential of a speedy and compact machine, with a high information-density and a complex operation—just what is needed by advanced computer applications such as virtual reality and artificial intelligence. These applications, which produce a more realistic interactive environment and more humanlike intelligence, exist today in electronic computers but have yet to reach their maximum potential.

But light and optics already plays a role in today's computational systems. Charge-coupled devices, discussed in chapter 9, have proven the value of light-sensing electrical circuits in cameras and telescopes, and modern computers have also adopted a combined optical and electrical nature—they store information in the form of optical discs.

CDs and DVDs

A CD or DVD is about 4.7 inches (120 mm) in diameter and a 1/20th of an inch (1.2 mm) thick. Both store information in a digital format,

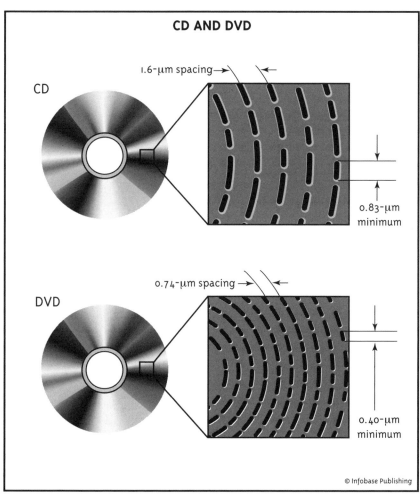

A portion of the track of a CD (top) and DVD (bottom)

as a series of pits as small as 0.000032 inches (0.8 μm) in a CD and half that size in a DVD, as illustrated in the figure on the previous page. The pits change the reflectance of the surface, and these changes represent a binary language that consists of a series of digits whose value is either 1 or 0. The digits encode music or computer data on a CD and movies or computer data on a DVD. The series of pits spirals around the disc to form a narrow track that is only 0.000064 inches (1.6 μm) wide in a CD and slightly less than half that in a DVD. The tiny tracks, if stretched out to their full length, would run more than 3.7 miles (5.9 km) for a CD and 7.5 miles (12 km) for a DVD. Manufacturers introduced dual discs in 2004, with one side formatted as a CD and the other side as a DVD.

DVDs have a higher information capacity than CDs because the pits are smaller. But even CDs require narrow, precise beams of light in order to measure the reflectance of the remarkably little structures. Ordinary light spreads out, and the pits would have to be much larger to be measured, but this would greatly reduce the storage capacity or require an impractically large disc. The only light that works is the coherent beam of a laser; semiconductor lasers, used in fiber optics, are also valuable for this function and are found in CD and DVD players.

If the pits could be made even smaller, more information could be stored on the same size disc. The problem is that the pits are about the same size as the wavelength of the laser light that illuminates them—for a DVD, this is typically about 0.000025 inches (640 nm) in the red portion of the spectrum. The thinness of the pits accounts for the colors produced by light reflecting from the underside of a CD or DVD, a behavior similar to thin films, as discussed in chapter 6. Anything much smaller than a light ray's wavelength has little effect on the ray, so the pits cannot be made smaller unless the wavelength of the illuminating light is smaller.

Some of the next generation of optical discs will increase the storage capacity by using lasers that make blue light instead of red. Blue light, with its smaller wavelength, can read smaller pits. Combined with other improvements, these Blu-ray discs can store five times as much information as a DVD—five movies on a single disc! Even single movies, if coded in a high-definition format that gives excellent resolution, are too information-dense for today's DVDs and require a higher capacity disc. Equipment using Blu-ray discs are already available in Japan (a country that makes a great deal of high-definition features) and appeared in the U.S. market in 2006.

Replacing Electrons with Photons

The heart of a computer today is its microprocessor—usually an integrated circuit that contains millions of electrical components such as transistors fashioned on a silicon chip the size of a quarter. The microprocessor is part of the central processing unit, where the computer performs calculations and processes the data. Transistors act like switches and form the circuits by which the calculations and processing are done, and a larger number of transistors provide a faster, higher-capacity machine. The electronics company Intel can make microprocessor chips containing more than 400 million transistors.

But there is a limit to how many transistors can be crammed onto a small chip. The miniaturization process is now beginning to reach a point where the components behave in a random, unpredictable fashion—the realm of quantum mechanics, which governs the behavior of atomic particles like electrons. Relatively big electrical circuits do not suffer from quantum mechanical effects because they use a lot of electrons; while individual electrons are unpredictable, the average behavior of a large number of them is predictable, and the circuits perform as expected. The problem arises when the transistors and circuits become small enough to involve only a few electrons.

Making the microprocessor is another problem with miniaturization. This difficulty is related to optics because manufacturers use ultraviolet radiation to etch the tiny components in the silicon. The wavelength and diffraction of light places restrictions on how small the components can be made.

For greater processing power, computer engineers may turn to photons. Electronic computers have many moving parts—even if they are only electrons—but a purely optical computer would have fewer. An optical computer could also be highly parallel—a structure that increases processing power because it allows a large number of computations to be performed at the same time. In this way, many different processes can occur in parallel, side by side, rather than occurring serially, one at a time. Light beams can pass right through one another without disruption, whereas electrical circuits must be separated. Different frequencies of light can also be used simultaneously, either collected together as "white light" or spread out into a spectrum. Optical computing can be incredibly small and fast, easily configured or reconfigured as necessary, suffer little from the effects of heating (as from electrical resistance), yet still have enough photons to make a reliable machine.

Faster computers would bring new and powerful applications. One important application is artificial intelligence, where computers display humanlike intelligence rather than just doing simple, programmed tasks. To make a computer more like a human brain, some engineers are designing artificial neural networks (ANNs); these networks consists of "cells" that are programmed to behave like brain cells, with connections between them to permit information processing that mimics the human brain. Many of these networks can learn by adjusting their properties, so that connections between "cells" change—just as they do in the real brain.

ANNs have been built with electronics devices but are somewhat limited. In order to compute like the brain, the cells must have a large number of connections, but this is difficult to accomplish in solid electrical devices. Optical neural networks, with cells that interact using light beams, avoid such limitations. Nabil Farhat, a professor at the University of Pennsylvania, has built simple networks using a system of light beams and electronic "cells." Sotaro Kawata and Akira Hirose of the University of Tokyo have explored the use of neural networks based almost entirely on optics, using semiconductor lasers and optical instruments. The phase of the light waves carries information, and the beams travel different paths, processing the data.

Controlling light is one of the difficulties of optical computing, whatever form it may ultimately take. Lenses and mirrors must be precise, and photons, unlike electrons, are hard to bottle up. But one researcher, Lene Vestergaard Hau, a physics professor at Harvard University, has developed the ability to manipulate the speed of light. As mentioned in the previous chapters, the speed of light is constant in a vacuum: 186,200 miles per second (300,000 km/s). Light slows when it travels through materials—the speed of light through many types of glass, for example, is about 124,000 miles per second (200,000 km/s) —but to slow down light even further, Professor Hau uses quantum mechanics.

The process begins with a tiny group of sodium atoms suspended and trapped by a magnetic field. By cooling the atoms to nearly the coldest possible temperature—absolute zero, –459.67°F or –273.15°C—their movements become sluggish, and they have low, ground-state energy. Researchers then send a pulse of light with the right frequencies to interact with the atoms. Researchers also shine another beam of light that mixes up the states of the system, according to the laws of quantum mechanics. Because of the interactions, each frequency of the light pulse meets with a different index of refraction, which causes them to travel at a different speed. The pulse gets blurred, and the group velocity falls drastically. In some experiments, Hau and her colleagues can even "freeze" light.

Slow light reduces one of the advantages of light—its speed—but the gains in controlling and processing the photons may offset this factor. Although quantum mechanics can disrupt small-scale systems because of its unpredictability, in some cases the strange effects, such as slowing light, are beneficial. The small size of these optical systems greatly decreases the length that light has to travel, so even the slowed photons can make the trip in an acceptable amount of time.

But optical computers are not going to arrive in the near future. The amazing devices produced by optical researchers rely on exceptionally difficult experiments and require a lot of time and expertise. There are also practical issues—a computer that needs to be maintained at a temperature near absolute zero is not coming to room-temperature households any time soon. Problems also arise when electronics comes in; a computer must interact with a human in order to be useful, and this generally requires electrical or mechanical devices that must mesh with the optics.

Yet with all the present and future difficulties, computing with light has a huge potential. Computers have gotten faster and better over the last few decades thanks to improvements in electronics, but limitations may reduce or even eliminate many of the next generation of applications. Photons, even if they must be slowed, are efficient messengers and processors of information.

14

MANUFACTURING OPTICAL INSTRUMENTS

Light's tiny wavelengths—0.000016–0.000028 inches (400–700 nm) —allow high-quality optical instruments to have excellent resolution but also require special care. A concave mirror focuses light to form the sharpest, highest resolution image only if the mirror is properly shaped and perfectly smooth on the scale of these wavelengths; any deviations scatter the rays and blur the image. The 94.5-inch (2.4-m) main mirror of NASA's *Hubble Space Telescope (HST)* took months of polishing and grinding, yet a major flaw 1/50th the diameter of a human hair resulted in serious focusing problems. Shortly after *HST* launched in 1990, astronomers discovered that its images were much poorer than expected.

Manufacturing precision optical instruments is a demanding task. The design of the *HST* mirror allowed little room for error, no greater than about a 1/20th of the wavelength of light, and this error was exceeded. Three and a half years after *HST*'s launch, astronauts on a space shuttle mission applied a fix, but it is always best to do the job right the first time. Meeting such stringent requirements takes special equipment, carefully controlled conditions, and spotlessly clean workrooms.

A Challenge of Precision

Small wavelengths, such as in X-rays or electrons used in the electron microscopes described in chapter 8, provide better resolution. This is why the National Institute of Standards (NIST), the U.S. agency devoted to precision measurements and defining the standard measuring units, developed XCALIBIR: X-ray Optics Calibration Interferometer. In its power, the machine resembles King Arthur's sword (Excalibur); using X-rays and interference fringes like those of the Michelson and Morley experiment discussed in chapter 3, XCALIBIR inspects optical surfaces with an exacting eye.

As mentioned in the previous chapter, the makers of tiny integrated circuit chips need remarkable precision, and XCALIBIR can help. The manufacturing process involves measuring the thickness and flatness of silicon wafers from which the chips are made, as well as lenses and mirrors to focus light—or ultraviolet radiation, for better resolution—in order to etch and configure the millions of components. XCALIBIR can determine the smoothness of 12-inch (30-cm) surfaces to within the diameter of a few atoms. Such accuracy benefits all kinds of optical work, and XCALIBIR has many applications, such as helping the National Ignition Facility, mentioned in chapter 11.

This kind of precision is not easy to achieve. XCALIBIR sits in a room that has a carefully controlled temperature; changes in temperature cause materials to change in size—this is called thermal expansion since the volume increases with heat—and XCALIBIR's enclosure must not depart from its normal temperature by 0.09°F (0.05°C), or the change in its size will throw off the measurements. Any sort of movement will also defeat the purpose, and the machine rests on a 16-ton granite block so that no vibrations will jar it while the delicate measurements are taking place.

Lack of accuracy causes problems such as that which plagued the *Hubble Space Telescope. HST*'s main mirror was an ambitious project, a large-sized mirror that was not meant to depart from its prescribed curvature by more than 0.00000125 inch (31.25 nm). The mirror consists of a special glass that does not change size much with temperature, and the reflecting surface has a coating of 0.000003 inches (75 nm) of pure aluminum, protected by another coating of 0.000001 inches (25 nm) of magnesium fluoride. But the edges of the great mirror were too flat, and the telescope suffered from spherical aberration. Since some of the light was not focused properly, the images were not as crisp as they should have been.

Scientists and engineers studied the problem, and on December 2, 1993, the space shuttle *Endeavour* rocketed up to *HST*'s 375-mile (600-km) orbit. The astronauts carried an optical system made by Ball Aerospace to correct the aberration; the system, called Corrective Optics Space Telescope Axial Replacement (COSTAR), contained several mirrors to adjust the path of the light and compensate for the flaw of the main mirror. The fix required several days of extravehicular activity by the shuttle's crew, who had needed special training in order to handle and install the optical equipment. The mission was a success and in January 1994, NASA displayed some much clearer images taken by the telescope.

Patience and Cleanliness

HST has made more than 400,000 observations on more than 25,000 objects, helping to answer questions on the birth and evolution of stars and the expansion of the universe. But the reliable machine is nearing the end of its lifetime, and NASA plans to launch another telescope, called the *James Webb Space Telescope* (*JWST*), in 2011. *JWST*'s main mirror will be about 256 inches (6.5 m) in diameter, but instead of one big piece, it will consist of 18 parts. This telescope will be able to detect objects that are 10 billion times fainter than the visible eye can see—dozens of times better in performance than the *Hubble Space Telescope*—with a resolution that could pick out Lincoln's beard on a penny from 24 miles (40 km) away. Making such an optical instrument requires a great deal of precision—and a lot of patience and cleanliness.

An object the size of *JWST*'s mirror would be too large to fit into the space available in a rocket, so the mirror will be made of 18 segments that are folded up until needed. The segments will be thin, lightweight beryllium mirrors. Beryllium (atomic number 4) is a metal with a lot of strength for its weight. Weight is a vital factor for launching objects into orbit, and an optical system this size would be too heavy to lift unless NASA carefully budgets the telescope's mass. Even though *JWST*'s mirror is several times larger than *HST*, the new space telescope will have about only half the mass of the old one.

JWST also has slightly different goals than *HST*. Astronomers plan to use the new space telescope to study the farthest galaxies; these galaxies are so far away that light takes billions of years to reach Earth. Because the universe is expanding, light from remote objects is shifted toward the lower frequencies due to the Doppler effect. (The Doppler effect is the same reason that the horn of a receding car or whistle of a receding train sounds lower in frequency.) The lower frequencies are toward the red end of the visible spectrum, and the farthest objects are so distant that a lot of their emissions are shifted to the infrared region. *JWST*'s optics will be configured to work best in the infrared portion of the spectrum, although the telescope will also make some observations with visible light.

Infrared is difficult for observatories to handle because everything glows in infrared, as discussed in chapter 10. In order to minimize its own infrared emissions, the telescope must operate at an extremely cold temperature: –364°F (–220°C). *JWST* will also be placed far away from infrared sources, about 1 million miles (1,600,000 km) away from Earth.

To fabricate, construct, and test a complicated and precise optical system like *JWST* requires years. Patience is also much in demand, so the *Hubble Space Telescope*'s error will not be repeated. Another part of the job is cleanliness—optical manufacturing at this delicate level cannot withstand even a slightly dusty environment.

Many industrial processes besides manufacturing optical instruments require the use of "clean rooms." Dust particles are present everywhere, as can be easily seen when a narrow shaft of light enters a house or building and illuminates hundreds of dancing motes. (The particles move due to air currents.) Small dust particles are a nuisance to sensitive noses but can mean disaster for the process of making integrated circuits and other computer components, as well as satellites, lenses, mirrors, and other optical devices. Contamination from dust particles can ruin a surface and disrupt a measurement, so the air of clean rooms must be controlled.

Clean room specifications describe the number of allowable dust particles of 0.0002 inch (0.5 μm) or larger per cubic foot of air. A class 1,000 clean room has no more than 1,000 such particles per cubic foot, and a class 100 has no more than 100. (Office buildings commonly have more than 500,000 particles per cubic foot.) To obtain strict standards of cleanliness, all aspects of the environment must be controlled: air flow, pressure, temperature, and humidity. Filters scrub the air, and fans and other devices circulate the air in certain directions, away from delicate equipment and processes. People working in clean rooms must follow strict procedures, and in the cleanest environments, personnel must wear special clothing that releases little lint and covers all of the skin (much dust in houses and offices comes from dead skin cells shed by the body).

Goddard Space Flight Center's clean room has a volume of 1,300,000 cubic feet (37,000 m³) and is one of the world's largest such rooms. [NASA]

Manufacturing optical instruments requires unerring precision and pristine environments, but the results are worth the effort. Many of the devices mentioned in the previous chapters would not have been possible without nearly perfect methods of construction. Making an instrument like the *James Webb Space Telescope* is a long and sometimes frustrating process, but the result is a thing of beauty—and allows people to see the farthest reaches of the universe.

OPTICS IN SCIENTIFIC RESEARCH

E arly 17th-century lens-makers aimed their telescopes seaward for a practical reason: They wanted to spot incoming fleets sooner than the ships could be seen with the unaided eye. When Galileo turned his telescope toward the sky, his purpose was scientific—to discover and study new phenomena—and he promptly found four new satellites of the planet Jupiter. Antoni van Leeuwenhoek had the same purpose in mind when he focused his microscope on drops of water and observed microorganisms of all shapes and descriptions. Other scientists followed their lead.

The microscope and telescope have revealed new worlds and unexpected phenomena to biologists and astronomers alike. This is a common occurrence throughout the history of all the sciences: New and improved instruments open new and fascinating avenues of exploration and study. Optical instruments have accomplished much in the service of science, shaping light to allow scientists see farther and more clearly than ever before.

Scientific research proceeds at a rapid pace today—there are more scientists working in university, industry, and government labs than at any other time in history—and optics continues to play a vital role. Researchers use optical instruments to create images of objects impossible to observe any other way, such as single molecules and gravitational waves. This chapter describes some of the most interesting optical tools in four different branches of science.

Optics and Chemistry

Scientists use spectroscopy to study the way substances emit or absorb light. Different substances are distinguishable by their distinct spectrum, as discussed in chapter 4 for the discovery of helium and the classification of stars. Spectroscopists can study any light, whether it is from a distant astronomical body or from a sample sitting on a laboratory bench, but normally they need a relatively large amount of material in order to gather enough light. One of the problems with this approach is that it obscures the behavior of single atoms or molecules.

Chemical experiments on material in bulk involve millions of particles and provide useful information on the aggregate properties but offer little data on how the individual components move or interact. Experiments on events occurring at the smallest scale, at the level of a few particles or just a single particle, are exceptionally difficult and in some cases impossible; yet the properties of single molecules affect many aspects of the material's behavior and activity. For instance, the structure of the molecule influences its participation in chemical reactions, and a catalysis—a molecule that speeds up the rate of a reaction—often needs to fit with the reactants in a specific orientation.

Optical microscopes have limited resolution, as discussed in chapter 8, and although electron microscopes have excellent resolution, they are not ideal for studying the spectral properties of molecules. But beginning in the 1980s, scientists found ways to "see" a single molecule and started using these methods of single molecule detection and spectroscopy to explore molecules of all sizes, from small inorganic compounds to huge biological molecules such as proteins and DNA. Chemists no longer needed millions of copies of the molecule in order to detect the presence of the substance or investigate its behavior.

Achieving single molecule sensitivity means limiting the spatial extent of the sample under study. This can be done by highlighting a small portion of the sample, similar to shining a stage spotlight on the star of the show. A laser, with its narrow, intense beam, is an excellent tool for this job. The energy of the beam excites a limited area, leaving the rest of the sample darkened and in the background. The light that is absorbed by this "star" of the show forms the subject of interest.

Even though a laser beam is narrow and coherent, it is still too wide to illuminate anything but a fairly large number of atoms and molecules. Rather than trying to isolate a particle in this tumultuous crowd, scientists prepare the sample before the experiment. The researchers dilute the molecules they want to examine, maintaining them in a floating or embedded state in a matrix of other material. The laser's wavelength must be chosen so that its light interacts strongly with the molecule of interest rather than the other material. If the matrix absorbs little or no light of the laser's wavelength, this material does not disturb the analysis.

Optics and Biology

Another technique of studying single molecules makes use of light but in a different way—an optical trap works by using light as a cage.

All beams of light exert a force. This force comes from the pressure of photons striking the surface of an object, similar to the way that air molecules of a breeze or wind push against objects. Winds can be tremendously strong, but the pressure of light, though it always exists when light shines on an object, is insignificant and unnoticeable in most situations. An exception to this rule occurs if the object is itself tiny—such as a single molecule—in which case photon pressure makes its presence felt.

Biologists study molecules that can be large strings of atoms, such as proteins consisting of thousands of atoms bonded together. Proteins perform a variety of complicated functions in cells and tissues of the body, even carrying cargo from one place to another by acting like a motor. Although large, a single molecule of protein is thousands of times thinner than a human hair, and these motors can exert only incredibly small forces. Studying these little protein motors is a difficult task, for there is no instrument small enough to take a direct measure of their activity.

One technique of studying particles such as these protein motors is to trap them in a beam of light. This is also no easy task, requiring an intense beam. One way to do it is to sandwich the molecule between two oppositely directed laser beams—the photons push in opposite directions, and if the forces are equal, the molecule goes nowhere.

Another type of optical trap keeps a particle steady with restoring forces. Photons have momentum and energy, and their interactions with matter obey the conservation laws. Due to the conservation of momentum, any object that changes the momentum of light by bending or reflecting it must experience an equal and opposite change in momentum. When a small particle finds itself in an intense beam of a laser, it can be trapped by a restoring force due to collisions with photons. Suppose the particle starts to move out of the beam; as the particle moves, it scatters photons out of the beam, and the collisions push the particle back into the beam, restoring its position. Although these forces are about a million times too weak to lift a grain of salt, they are enough to confine a molecule. Light makes an excellent cage for biological molecules because it has such a soft touch, and delicate structures suffer no serious damage. Some molecules may be damaged by exposure to visible light, but infrared beams will often work just as well.

A basic optical trap, as shown in the figure below, involves a laser beam focused by a high-quality lens, such as the objective lens of an expensive microscope. This tightens the laser beam into a pinpoint of light that holds the molecule within its center. These instruments are also known as optical tweezers and can often manipulate the trapped molecule with electromagnetic fields or other forces. Optical traps are usually not combined with single molecule spectroscopy because of the intense light required by the trap.

The molecular motors studied by biologists do not function as a group but act alone, and optical traps or tweezers are excellent tools to study these miniature movers one at a time. Proteins such as kinesin and dynein use the energy of a compound called adenosine triphosphate to transport globular membranes filled with important mol-

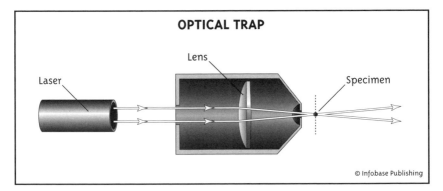

OPTICAL TRAP

Lens

Laser

Specimen

© Infobase Publishing

The lens focuses the laser on the specimen, a tiny particle trapped in the beam.

ecules. Biologists have determined that these tiny motors "walk" along fibers by attaching and reattaching part of the molecule in a series of steps, each exerting a tiny force that carries the mover and cargo forward at a pace of up to 10 inches (25 cm) a day.

Optics and Physics

Electromagnetic radiation can make traps for small molecules or be helpful in the analysis of their structure, as in spectroscopy, but sometimes radiation itself is the subject of research. Physicists are beginning to explore a little known realm in the spectrum called terahertz.

People commonly encounter visible light, infrared, and ultraviolet frequencies of electromagnetic radiation, and radio and X-rays are also easily produced. The portion of the spectrum between 100 gigahertz (billion hertz) and 10 terahertz (trillion hertz) is not nearly as common. As a result, this terahertz range, which has an energy greater than microwave radiation but less than infrared, is unexplored territory.

But improved sources of terahertz have recently been developed and exploited, giving physicists a glimpse into this region. Machines that accelerate small particles to speeds close to that of light sometimes generate significant quantities of terahertz radiation, and terahertz-emitting lasers have also been developed, with a medium consisting of indium, gallium, and arsenic; or silicon and germanium; or other combinations of elements. Using these sources gives scientists a chance to study large amounts of the radiation. For example, scientists at Rensselaer Polytechnic Institute in Troy, New York, have built a large facility devoted to research on terahertz.

Although all forms of electromagnetic radiation share similar properties, different frequencies make them unique and useful for their own particular applications. In the late 19th century, Hertz studied electromagnetic radiation by producing radio waves, a type of wave that soon became critical in telecommunications. A few years later, Röntgen discovered and studied X-rays, a high-energy radiation that immediately found use in medical imaging. Terahertz will also have special purposes, particularly since these waves are often involved in the emission and absorption spectra of molecules. This makes terahertz spectroscopy important for probing the structure and internal motion of molecules, with the advantage that the lower energies of this radiation do little damage compared to X-rays and other high-energy techniques.

Potential applications for terahertz include taking "pictures" of concealed material or objects. For example, water in the leaf of a plant effects the transmission of terahertz radiation, so a measurement of how much terahertz passes through is an indication of the water content. Mapping the distribution of this vital liquid at different times helps agricultural scientists to understand how a plant uses water in the process of growth and development. Terahertz may also find use in police and security operations since terahertz can locate a weapon hidden in a newspaper or other material—the paper blocks light and the weapon cannot be seen, but terahertz burrows through and can be used to form an image, similar to an X-ray image of a bone.

Optics and Astronomy

Astronomers, who deal with the whole universe and often must attempt to see—and think—big, rely on optics to bring them information from distant bodies in space. As mentioned in chapter 10, this includes all parts of the electromagnetic spectrum. An ambitious NASA project called LISA hopes to extend the vision of astronomers to include other waves, with the aid of lasers and the power of optics.

Gravity is one of the forces of nature and, like electromagnetism, physicists believe that gravitational waves carry its energy, just as light carries the energy of electromagnetic fields. Although gravity is one of the most important forces for people on Earth, in terms of physics it is a meager force—electromagnetism is astoundingly stronger, by a factor of about 10^{39}. Gravity is also a mysterious force, and physicists are still uncertain how it fits with the other forces of nature (which include electromagnetism, the strong nuclear force, and the weak nuclear force). By studying gravitational waves that theoretically exist—but have not yet been directly detected, probably due to their tiny amplitude—physicists will achieve a clearer understanding of this puzzling force.

LISA stands for Laser Interferometer Space Antenna. The plan involves the development and launch into deep space of three identical spacecraft in a cooperative effort by scientists and engineers at NASA and the European Space Agency. Ground-based searches for gravitational waves have been performed but are difficult—the existence of the planet, along with all its vibrations, hamper the process, a problem that the space-based LISA would avoid. But being in space presents problems of a different sort, and currently LISA exists only on the drawing board.

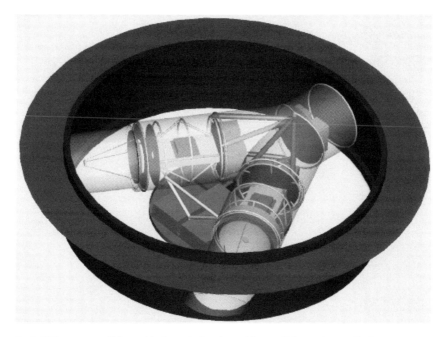

Each LISA spacecraft has a Y-shaped structure. The craft is made mostly from a graphite-epoxy compound. [NASA/JPL-Caltech]

The three spacecraft that will compose LISA have the shape of a short cylinder, 5.9 feet (1.8 m) in diameter and 1.57 feet (0.48 m) long. Solar panels absorb the energy of the Sun and provide power. Each of the craft contains several items: a laser, an 11.8-inch (30-cm) telescope to help transmit and receive laser signals, and the test masses that provide the gravitational reference sensor.

LISA will use interferometry to detect gravitational waves. The three craft will be positioned to form an equilateral triangle—a triangle with equal sides and angles—and together they will create a large-scale version of the interferometer used by Michelson and Morley, as discussed in chapter 3. Michelson and Morley compared the speed of light along different paths by measuring the wave interference of the beams; a change in speed of one of the beams would have changed their relative phase, showing up as light and dark bands when the beams overlapped at the end of the journey. LISA will find gravitational waves by measuring a change in distance between the craft as the wave rolls through their triangular geometry.

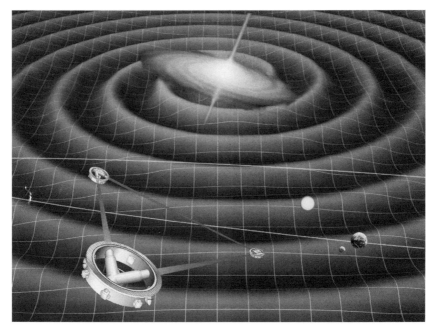

Scientists hope that LISA will be able to detect gravitational waves rippling through space. [NASA/JPL-Caltech]

The lasers provide coherent beams of light that travel between the craft, which will be separated by about 3,125,000 miles (5,000,000 km). The craft "float" in space, and aboard each are highly polished objects—the test masses—that reflect the laser beams. A beam of one craft shoots to and from the other two, and when combined in a detector the difference in path, if any, shows up as interference bands; the path to and from the other spacecraft act like two arms of the Michelson and Morley interferometer. Since each of LISA's three vessels can transmit and receive laser signals, all have interferometry capability.

Because gravitational waves are so weak, LISA requires a great deal of precision. Disturbances from the solar wind—a small but steady stream of particles emitted by the Sun—and drifting of the craft must be avoided or detected and corrected. The designed plan includes tiny jets called microthrusters to maintain perfect alignment and distance of the three cylinders. The sensors of the craft must be shielded from electromagnetism to prevent movement due to this powerful force, which would overwhelm the gravitational effect. What LISA will attempt to measure are the distortions in space itself as the gravitational waves roll by, and to do that LISA will have the incredible ability to measure any change in the craft distances to within 1/10th the size of a single atom.

Funding for LISA is not certain, and budget constraints are a concern. But if the project proceeds as planned, launch will occur in 2015, and the mission will last five years.

This chapter presented only a sample of the uses of light and optics in scientific research. In some ways, optics is involved in every endeavor—the eye and vision are usually critical sources of information—but the illumination afforded by optical instruments gives an extra advantage. From the study of single molecules to research conducted in the vastness of space, optics has aided and will continue to aid scientific discovery.

16

OPTICS IN MEDICINE: IMPROVING SURGICAL PROCEDURES AND LIFTING MOOD

The earliest applications of many branches of science are in some way related to health and the treatment of disease. Roman physicians prescribed headache remedies that involved electricity, a mysterious force emitted by fish such as the torpedo—a species of fish capable of generating a pain-numbing shock. Chemists in the Middle Ages mixed their elements and compounds and searched for antiaging potions. Early optics had its uses in medicine as well, such as magnifying glasses to inspect wounds.

Physicians in ancient Rome also advised people to live in houses with an abundance of sunlight. This recommendation benefited a person's eyes, providing plenty of light with which to see, but had another advantage: The bright light lifted mood. Perhaps people throughout history have always been at least vaguely aware of the effects of an outdoor stroll on a bright, sunny day, and modern science supports these beliefs.

The power of light to heal has made many advances along with the science of optics. Part of the electromagnetic spectrum known as X-rays have been used to image the body, especially the bones, ever since Wilhelm Röntgen made his discovery in 1895, but electromagnetic radiation closer in frequency to visible light is also important. Today artificial lights mimic sunlight and flexible fiber optics extends a doctor's vision into a patient's gastrointestinal tract. Lasers provide valuable service to medicine in many different fields, and physicians who enlist these narrow beams of energy to cut or sculpt tissue know that lasers make fine scalpels.

Surgical Lasers

Physicians can use lasers in almost any surgical procedure. Although lasers are generally expensive and require specialized training to maintain and operate, they offer advantages over sharp cutting tools such as scalpels and electrical devices. The beam of the laser can be precisely controlled, so the surgeon can use a high-intensity laser to cut tissue exactly where required, and the heat seals off blood vessels so there is less bleeding. Surgical lasers decrease the risk of infection, minimize the discomfort a patient experiences after an operation, and in some cases reduce the extent of the procedure.

Lasers can not only cut, but they can also burn tissue if applied over a larger area. This technique has become extremely popular recently for several types of procedures. One of these procedures involves the improvement of eyesight.

Chapter 7 discussed the eye and how the lens and cornea bend light to focus an image on the retina. The cornea does most of the bending, while muscles shape the lens to make small adjustments. In many people, the eye does a less than perfect job because the cornea is not the right shape, or the eyeball is elongated or flattened. Vision for these people is blurry and out of focus unless they wear prescription eyeglasses or contact lenses.

Although glasses and lenses work, they are sometimes a bother to wear. A better method of correcting vision would be to correct the eye itself, sculpting the cornea to the right shape for the person's eyeball. This would involve cutting or burning thin slices of tissue from the cornea in order to create the best geometry for producing a clear, crisp image on the retina.

Surgeons have used exceptionally thin knives to reshape corneas, but lasers are ideal tools for the task. One of the most common procedures is called LASIK, which stands for laser-assisted in situ keratomileusis. *In situ* means the operation is performed with the eye in its normal position, and *keratomileusis* refers to the shaping of the cornea tissue. Physicians use computers to calculate the necessary contour and to control the beam during the operation; the laser is commonly an excimer laser that has an ultraviolet beam. Excimer lasers get their energy from excited dimers—when pumped, the medium of these lasers contain chemicals that bind together and create compounds called dimers, which generate the population inversion needed for the laser's operation.

Not everyone with vision problems is a good candidate for this kind of surgery. The best patient is an older person whose eyewear prescription has been constant for the last few years; this means the person's eyesight and the problems associated with it are stable. A laser procedure such as LASIK is permanent, and if the person's eye and vision continue to change, the new shape will no longer be the right shape. Young people in particular are not good candidates because growth and maturity often changes their eye and vision, and most physicians will not perform LASIK surgery on anyone under 18 years of age.

For patients who meet the requirements, LASIK offers hope of a reduction in the patient's dependence on corrective eyewear. The surgery is quick, finishing in 30 minutes or less, and is one of the most popular elective (nonessential) surgeries. Although most patients do not come away with perfect vision, LASIK surgeries often result in significant vision improvement, and each year, more than a million patients in the world undergo the procedure.

Another popular laser-assisted surgery is for vanity instead of vision—and also common only among the older crowd.

Light at Work on the Skin

Over time, the smooth skin of youthful faces gradually gives way to wrinkles. During aging, skin slowly loses its elasticity—the ability to snap back into place and return to its original position—and deposits of fatty tissue replace muscles. The skin sags, and creases that accompany facial expressions such as a smile or frown do not go away when the expression fades, but instead remain as permanent lines in the skin of the forehead, cheeks, and around the eyes.

Although to some people the aging process is a mark of distinction and character, other people find these unmistakable signs of their lost youth to be unattractive. Attempts to restore a youthful appearance often involve plastic surgery, also known as cosmetic surgery. One of the more popular operations is commonly called a face-lift—the technical term is *rhytidectomy*—in which a surgeon makes small incisions and lifts the skin from the underlying fat and muscle tissue. After suctioning some of the fat from the face and neck and tightening the muscle, the surgeon trims the excess skin and closes the incisions with stitches. If the operation is successful, the patient's face does not sag as much and is more youthful.

But the old skin remains. A way of getting rid of some of the wrinkles is to "peel" the skin away and let new skin grow in its place. A popular method of accomplishing this peel or resurfacing procedure is with a laser.

The laser, often a CO_2 laser, removes the thin, top layers of skin, similar to the way the excimer lasers sculpt the cornea. The treatment lasts anywhere from a few minutes to more than an hour, depending on the size of the area to be treated. In the process of healing and recovery from the peeling, the body grows new layers of skin as cells divide and take the place of the lost tissue. The new skin is generally smoother than the old, resulting in a new and more youthful surface. Laser resurfacing can also help with scars and uneven coloring of the skin. Lasers are a relatively new tool for this procedure, which is also performed by chemicals or mild abrasives. Because lasers are new, the advantages and disadvantages of this technique as compared to the alternatives are not yet clear.

Hair removal is another cosmetic procedure in which lasers are useful. To those people whose taste in fashion includes an absence of body hair, lasers deliver energy into the skin and kill the unwanted hair follicles. This technique offers a longer-lasting though more expensive alternative to a shaving razor or the unpleasant though effective use of wax.

Light as Emotional Therapy

Light does more than deliver energy to the surface of the body or provide information to the eyes for vision. Light affects the brain in more ways than just the visual sense.

As discussed in chapter 7, the human visual system contains cells that respond to different wavelengths of light, which the person sees as different colors. Colors play many roles in today's society. For example, since bright yellow or red captures people's attention so readily, fire engines and other emergency vehicles that need high visibility display these colors.

Colors in nature tend to be associated with specific environments: Earth tones such as green are linked with vegetation and spring; blue is the color of the sky and the ocean; and red, yellow, and orange shades are frequently found in ripe fruit. Over the span of generations, the human brain and its neural networks have grown accustomed to these associations to the extent that these colors can affect a person's mood and emotions. "Warm" colors such as orange and red are stimulating, while "cool" colors such as blue and green are calming. Many retail businesses decorate their store walls with warm colors because they tend to produce more sales than cool colors, and fast-food restaurants use red, orange, and brown in the attempt to stimulate their customers to eat briskly and leave—making room for the next group.

One of the authors of this book (Kyle Kirkland) observes the mood effects of colors on each of his semiannual visits to the dentist. Most of the rooms of his dentist's office mix calming colors with pictures of pleasant country scenes, such as mountain meadows or lakes. The reduction in anxiety is noticeable, particularly to a person who views a dental appointment with the same attitude he would have if thrown into a nest of pit vipers.

White light, as from the Sun, also has strong effects. Bright light exposure is important for a number of reasons, both in terms of biology and psychology. Sunshine stimulates the production of vitamin D, for instance, and bright, sunny days elevate mood. Bright light is even effective in treating mood disorders such as *seasonal affective disorder* (SAD).

SAD is a type of depression that strikes people in the sunlight-deprived fall or winter seasons and lasts until the following spring. It is a common disorder, affecting about 5 percent of the population, and results in sadness, withdrawal, irritability, and a lack of energy. Psychologists began studying light as a therapy for SAD in the mid-1980s, and over the course of the last two decades, research generally confirms its effectiveness. In 2005, a review commissioned by the American Psychiatric Association found that light therapy works as well for SAD as antidepressant drugs. Light therapy has also been effective in treating other, nonseasonal episodes of mild depression.

Unlike people located at more northerly latitudes, sunbathers in Hawaii can be exposed to bright light and work on their tans year-round. [Kyle Kirkland]

Patients treated with light therapy receive exposure to a bright light for about a half-hour every day, usually during the early morning. A light box, usually containing fluorescent tubes behind a plastic screen, produces a light with about the same intensity as an early summer morning or evening—perhaps 1/10th as strong as the noon Sun. Although the light is white like sunlight—meaning it has all the colors of the spectrum—filters remove the ultraviolet radiation, as it poses a risk and does not seem to be necessary for an effective treatment. The procedure usually continues through the winter, ending only when spring arrives.

The reason why light therapy works is not yet understood. Light is known to have effects on circadian (daily) rhythms, and there are cells and networks in the brain that use light received through the eyes to maintain the pace of these rhythms. (Traveling across time zones often disrupts circadian rhythms for a short period of time and makes a person feel out of sync—this is sometimes called jet lag.) Light therapy may affect areas of the brain related to these processes, along with other networks that govern mood, appetite, and sleep.

Other Uses of Medical Optics

In addition to laser surgery and the mood-elevating influence of intense light, optics has found other ways to serve medicine. One of these devices belongs in the simple, old-fashioned category of providing better vision—but of places that physicians were not able to visually inspect before.

An endoscope is a thin tube made of fiber optics and a high-quality lens, used by physicians to view cavities or organs of a patient's body. The physician guides the device as it snakes into openings like the mouth or small incisions made by a surgeon. Endoscopes have two optical fibers: One fiber carries light to illuminate the dark interiors of the body, and the other returns the reflected light and routes it through a lens to create an image. The part of the endoscope inserted into the patient's body may be flexible or it may be rigid, depending on if it needs to make sharp turns (as it does if the endoscope must follow the winding passage of the intestine). Besides the optical fibers, endoscopes may be outfitted with openings to inject drugs, or they may have foldable instruments such as scissors to make incisions or provide tissue samples. The image generated by the lens may be projected on a video screen for easier viewing or recorded on tape or DVD.

Endoscopes made with fiber optics were one of the earliest applications of fiber technology, gaining common use in the 1960s. Earlier endoscopes allowed physicians to peer into the body's passageways, but the instruments were either rigid or only partially flexible, limiting the view while at the same time occasionally posing a risk of serious injury. The thin, flexible glass of fiber optics—the same equipment used to transmit large volumes of data on the Internet—is ideal for endoscopy, explaining its rapid adoption.

The images acquired with endoscopes help physicians to diagnose a number of disorders or conditions within the body, and in some cases, endoscopes also become involved in the treatment. Endoscopes allow physicians to detect and monitor such conditions as ulcers of the stomach, abnormal bleeding, gallbladder stones, polyps (abnormal growths), abscesses (collections of pus due to infection), and inflammation. Physicians may also do a biopsy (gather a tissue sample for testing) with an endoscope or perform repair procedures such as the removal of damaged cartilage from a joint.

Before the development of fiber-optic endoscopes, many conditions or diseases occurring inside the body could be dealt with only by surgery: Physicians had to perform a procedure known as exploratory surgery, opening and probing the body in order to determine what was wrong with the patient. Surgery is risky and invites infection, and endoscopy, although not without risk, is much simpler, safer, and can be accomplished quickly and usually without the need for admission to a hospital—so the patient can return home or to work a short period of time later.

Flexible endoscopes are excellent tools and equip doctors with "eyes" at the end of stalks, significantly enhancing vision and making their lives, and those of their patients, much easier. There is even a possibility that the stalks could be extended to long distances that permit remote procedures; in these cases, the physician need not be present at the operation!

Light and its many facets are crucial to medicine. Light is a medium of information and of mood or emotion, and at high intensity, it is strong enough to cut, sculpt, and peel. Advances in optics have resulted in great improvements in diagnostic and surgical procedures, and perhaps one day, optics will carry a health provider's vision all the way across the globe.

OPTICS IN ART
AND ILLUSIONS

When the ancient Romans visited the British Isles, they discovered warriors who wore paint on their bodies. The paint may have served a number of purposes, including artistic and medicinal, as well as intimidatory—it made the warriors look fiercer. Many historians believe the word *Britain* derives from a Celtic word for painted.

The importance of painting goes even further back in time. For some unknown reason, people as far back as 30,000 years ago went to considerable trouble to make colored drawings on the walls of caves. The drawings, like the 20,000-year-old cave art in Lascaux, France, often depict animals such as bison. These paintings may have been art for art's sake, or they may have also had a religious or ceremonial purpose, but whatever the reason, it is clear that the urge to draw has been with people for a long time.

Light and optics are involved in many aspects of art and painting. The process of depicting a three-dimensional world on a two-dimensional canvas is not easy, and making the picture seem real requires an understanding of light, color, and geometry. The painting has only two dimensions, but the viewer must be made to see three, one of which is present only in the viewer's mind. Optics is

The urge to create a work of art is strong, particularly when the artist has something important to say. [Kyle Kirkland]

useful in understanding how things can appear to be what they are not, both in art and in illusions.

Pigments and Dyes

Since color is so important to humans, even artists in early times tried to make colorful pictures. These artists obviously could not buy supplies from an art store, so they made their paint by mixing colored compounds with spit or animal fat. The process was similar to the way paint is still made today. Paint consists of some colored substance, a pigment, suspended or mixed with some sort of medium. In ancient times, the pigments included charcoal, which produced black shades, and iron oxides, which produced red or orange shades. Today a large number of pigments of almost any imaginable color can be found, and the medium is often oil, egg yolk, or acrylic. When an artist applies the paint, the medium dries or undergoes a process of chemical hardening, and the pigment becomes trapped and sticks to the surface, whether it is a cave wall or a heavy piece of paper.

Dyes are also substances used to color objects. A dye is usually in a transparent solution—dissolved in water—unlike pigments, the small solid particles of paint that are held in a fluid or soft substance. Dyes have always been important in the making of clothes. The ancient Phoenicians were an industrious people and excellent mariners, and they extracted a dye called Tyrian purple from shellfish. Crushing the shells of these creatures yielded a fluid that turned purple once it had been applied to a cloth fiber and exposed to air. Since thousands of shells made only a pitiful amount of dye, the process was hugely expensive, and only a few people had enough money to buy it. Tyrian purple became the dye of royalty because they were the only ones who could afford it.

Unlike Tyrian purple, blue dye was not so scarce in ancient times. Blue could be obtained by using indigo from tropical plants such as *Indigofera tinctoria* or by using a less vivid but cheaper dye derived from a plant commonly called woad (*Isatis tinctoria*). The leaves of the woad plant contained a substance that could be turned into a dye after much processing using mixtures with unpleasant ingredients, including urine. This is the blue dye that may have decorated the warriors seen by the Romans in the British Isles.

Indigo was rare in Europe, imported for thousands of years in costly trading with India and other distant countries. But with improved transportation, the blue dye from indigo became more common. In the past century and a half, indigo has found widespread use in a certain type of attire: blue jeans, billions of which around the world have been made and dyed. Since indigo fails to bond strongly to the cloth, time and the washing machine slowly remove the dye—which makes another piece of attire, faded blue jeans.

Pigments and dyes are colored but have different properties than colored lights, as described in chapter 6. A colored light is electromagnetic radiation of a certain wavelength, but a substance gets its color, if it has any, by absorbing some of the wavelengths of light striking it and reflecting the rest. If white light strikes an apple, for instance, the long wavelengths of visible light—in the "red" part of the spectrum—reflect most strongly. While a white object reflects all wavelengths about equally and a black object absorbs most wavelengths (reflecting a small amount of each), a colored object reflects only a subset—this is what makes it have a color to the human eye.

The mixing of colors is also different with pigments and dyes than with lights. Combining lights of different colors is called additive mixing because each colored light adds wavelengths to the mixture.

Combining pigments is called subtractive mixing—instead of adding wavelengths, each pigment takes some away from the reflected light since pigments are colored by absorbing certain wavelengths. This makes combinations of light behave differently than pigments or dyes; red, green, and blue light combine to produce white light, but paints of the same colors mix to a muddy brown.

For additive mixing, red, green, and blue are called *primary colors* because all colors can be generated from some combination of these lights, and the three together produce uncolored, white light. In subtractive mixing, this combination of paint absorbs most wavelengths, and so appears dark brown. While televisions, which of course produce light, use combinations of red, green, and blue to make color, color printing is a subtractive process, and printers obtain the best mixing with cyan, magenta, and yellow. (Most printers also have black ink, the fourth color of "four-color printing," since a mixture of cyan, magenta, and yellow does not yield an adequately dark color.)

Mixing colors is not a new idea. Robin Hood and his merry men apparently could not get their hands on green dye, so to make their green uniforms, they first dyed them blue (probably from woad) and then used a yellow dye. The mixture yielded the desired result.

Until the 19th century, dyes were natural substances. Then in the 1850s, a teenaged British chemist, William Perkin, accidentally discovered a concoction that dyed cloth an elegant purple. Perkin built a business around this synthesized substance, which he called mauveine. The dye became popular in the latter half of the 19th century when its mauve color was the height of fashion. But this dye was just the beginning, and today painters and dyers have thousands of artificial dyes and pigments from which to choose.

Depth and Perspective

Color adds interest to a painting, but a flat, two-dimensional picture seems false because the world has three dimensions: up and down, left and right, backward and forward. The first two—the vertical and horizontal dimensions—can be captured on a flat surface; the third dimension, depth, can only be hinted at or imitated.

As discussed in chapter 7, people get their depth perception from having two eyes instead of just one. Separated by a distance of about 2.5 inches (6.3 cm), the two eyes give slightly different views, and the brain combines them to make a single, three-dimensional image in

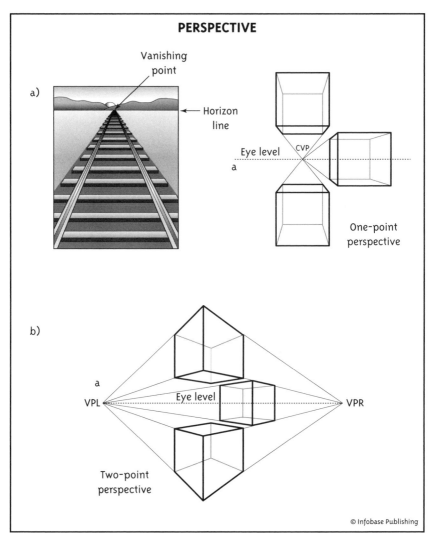

PERSPECTIVE

a) Vanishing point

Horizon line

Eye level

CVP

a

One-point perspective

b) a

VPL — Eye level — VPR

Two-point perspective

© Infobase Publishing

(a) Parallel lines that recede in the distance, like the pair of rails of a railroad, converge to a point, the vanishing point. When the edges of the cubes are extended with imaginary lines, they also converge to a vanishing point. This is one-point perspective. (b) When the cubes are drawn at an angle, imaginary lines extending from the edges form two vanishing points. This is two-point perspective.

the "mind's eye." A person with normal vision sees depth—objects are extended in space, and some objects are closer than others.

Although much of a person's depth perception depends on combining two different views from the eyes, this is not the only basis for perceiving depth. Other clues are available, and people readily use them to perceive depth—particularly people who must rely on only a single eye. Many of these clues can be rendered on a flat surface, so artists use them to hint at the third dimension—the illusion of depth—in the drawings.

Linear perspective is a method of illustrating the relationship between size and distance. As shown in part (a) of the figure, the parallel lines of a railroad track converge to a single point in the far distance. This is true of any set of parallel lines that extend for great lengths from the observer—the lines meet at a point on the horizon. This point is called a vanishing point, since the lines seem to converge and disappear. The blocks in the figure show that the outline of multiple objects, if viewed from the same side, form a set of lines that would also converge at a distance, if imaginary extensions were drawn from them.

The point of convergence is at the same level as the observer's eye. This level is the horizon, providing the observer has an unobstructed view of his or her surroundings. When looking at the ocean, for example, the sky and water meet at the horizon. In cities or mountainous terrain, the horizon seems higher because objects are blocking the view, but the vanishing point for the imaginary extensions of buildings and similar structures is usually at the eye-level horizon.

The wall illustrates one-point perspective as its height seems to diminish with distance. [Kyle Kirkland]

The corner of this building illustrates two-point perspective. Both sides seem to decrease with distance, and the edges of each side would meet at a different vanishing point if the building were long enough. [Kyle Kirkland]

If the artist draws objects that recede or shrink with distance into a vanishing point (or the imaginary lines extending from these objects do so), this gives a picture an illusion of depth. When the objects of a painting or drawing show only a single side to the viewer, the lines converge into a single vanishing point—this is one-point perspective, as illustrated by the blocks in part (a) of the figure on page 144. When the artist draws corners or angles, the lines or imaginary lines extend toward two vanishing points, as shown in part (b) of the figure. This is two-point perspective. In a picture that shows a lot of vertical objects, there is yet another vanishing point, although this point would probably be high in the sky and far beyond the page. Vanishing points for pictures that depict only close objects, such as an indoor scene, may also be located well off the page of the drawing, but the artist knows they are there and draws accordingly.

Linear perspective is a way of showing how objects decrease in size with distance, but there are other effects of distance and depth besides size, and these effects offer more techniques and tricks for an artist. One of the most obvious is occlusion—one object in front of another covers, or occludes, the more distant object. Another clue comes from atmospheric distortion: The atmosphere scatters blue light, and objects at a great distance appear a grayish blue.

An object's texture is also a clue to distance. Up close, the surface of a boulder may be grainy, pocked, or dabbed with dirt, but at a distance, those features disappear, and the boulder's surface appears uniformly smooth. The diminished size caused by great distance means that the small details or features—the texture—of a surface disappears, so even if an object is visible from a long way off, its characteristics are different than when the object is near the viewer.

An important clue to depth and distance in an image is occlusion, the blocking of one object by another. In this picture, the fence is clearly in front of the tree, which is in front of the buildings in the background that form part of Philadelphia's skyline. [Kyle Kirkland]

This picture of the coauthor, Kyle Kirkland, in Hawaii shows a dark, nearby hill on the left and a far more distant hill—belonging to another island—on the right. The atmosphere makes the distant island appear light grayish in color, much lighter in tone than the nearby hill. [Elizabeth Kirkland]

Skilled artists translate depth into linear perspective and distance clues in their flat-surfaced pictures, giving the illusion of three dimensions when there are only two. This skill is not simple and developed in European culture during the Renaissance—only after people began to study and understand optics and the behavior of rays of light. Some of the best artists during the Renaissance also were some of the best scientists and engineers. Leonardo da Vinci (1452–1519) is famous for his art—the *Mona Lisa*, for example—as well as his remarkably accurate anatomical drawings and his imaginative investigation on the nature of flight.

The Renaissance artists were among the first to use perspective correctly. People marvel at these old paintings, and there is a theory today, promoted by artist David Hockney, that the Renaissance painters actually used lenses or mirrors to trace outlines of the scenes to help them achieve the right look. This theory is controversial, and some scholars object to the idea that the great master artists used such aids, but the fact remains that a knowledge of optics was essential. People had been drawing on cave walls and coarse canvas for thousands of years before geometrical optics, and the careful observations of people interested in light could perfect the artist's illusion of depth.

Today's artists continue the tradition. The work of a young artist named Doug Braithwaite, for example, has appeared in galleries from coast to coast. His outdoor landscape paintings capture the rich colors and contrasts of the environment and the atmosphere.

Water on the Road and Other Mirages

Optical illusions are not limited to painters. The Müller-Lyon illusion, shown in the figure below, illustrates an optical illusion. The two lines are the same length, but the arrows on the ends create the mistaken impression in many people that one of the lines—the one with the arrows pointed inward—is longer. A ruler or measuring tape is not fooled.

An illusion is a deception. Like depth in a two-dimensional picture, illusions are in the mind of the observer, created by the brain's attempts to understand what it sees. The Müller-Lyon illusion, for

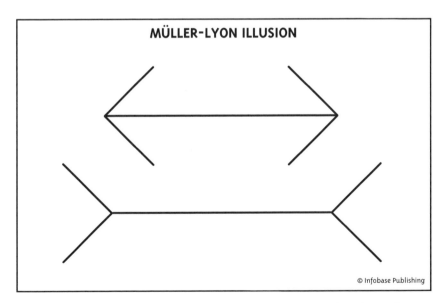

The bottom line, with the arrows pointing inward, seems longer than the top line, whose arrows point outward. A ruler shows they are the same length.

example, may fool people because the inward arrows stick out from the line, making the line appear longer. Another possible explanation is that the line with the inward arrows seems longer because it appears to be jutting out from the page. If this is the case, then the brain may be correctly measuring the length of the two lines—they are equal—but it gets fooled because it believes one line is closer, and this line therefore should appear bigger.

Even though people may not be consciously aware of it, the brain knows quite a lot about size and distance, and it adjusts visual perception accordingly. The image of an object makes a certain size on the retina, smaller when the object is far and bigger when near, but the brain knows that the object's real size is constant. The brain can use the depth clues mentioned earlier and estimate distances. As a result, an object may appear its "right" size to a person's perception even if it makes a small image on the retina, because the brain compensates for the effects of distance.

There is another aspect of vision that causes people's perception to differ from reality. In illusions, it is the brain that plays the trick, but

The image of the small boat on the left in this photograph is about the same size as the distant cruise ship in the center, but the human brain and visual system realizes that the cruise ship is actually much larger. [Elizabeth Kirkland]

at other times, nature is the guilty party. A mirage is a real optical phe-nomenon—it is not a deception or a case where the brain mistakes one thing for another, for mirages can be photographed. But a mirage is an illusion in the sense that it represents something whose appearance is different or altered from what is really there.

Mirages occur because of atmospheric refraction. They often happen because of unusual conditions in the atmosphere, such as the formation of layers of cold or warm air. The temperature differences in warm and cold air create a difference in density—warm air rises because it is less dense, as the higher temperature causes the air mol-ecules to move quickly and expand. This density difference produces a boundary, an interface between two substances just like an interface between glass and air. The boundary between warm and cold air is not usually as straight or rigid as other boundaries, but it behaves the same way with regard to the passage of light: Refraction takes place, since light travels at a slightly different speed in cold, dense air.

Air boundaries can cause mirages when the light coming from a distance object, beyond the horizon, bends along with the curvature of the planet's surface. The object then appears as if it were eerily floating above the horizon. If the temperature boundary that causes the refrac-tion is curved, the boundary can act as a lens, magnifying the image and inverting it. A mirage of a ship, which is actually sailing beyond the viewer's horizon and out of a direct line of sight, may suddenly appear to be floating upside down above the water. Many stories of ghost ships may have their origins in such mirages.

A more common mirage occurs in summer, when the Sun heats the ground, and the air just above the surface becomes extremely hot. This air forms a boundary with cooler air above, strong enough to bend the light rays coming downward from the sky so that they skim around the surface or even nudge upward again. Light from the sky is blue, and to a viewer, these refracted rays have the appearance of water. In deserts, cruel mirages tempt thirsty travelers into chasing an oasis that seems to lie ahead but can never be reached.

The common water-on-the-road mirage belongs in the same category. The Sun heats the asphalt, and the air above becomes hot, refracting light from the sky. The shimmering pool that motorists see in the road in front of them is really the sky, not water. Even animals can be fooled. In 2004, a group of brown pelicans lost their way and ended up in Arizona where many were injured because they tried to dive into a road and found a much harder surface than they expected.

Although some mirages produce unpleasant surprises or even disastrous results, not all mirages and illusions are bad. Optical phenomena obey the laws of physics, and an understanding of these laws generated many of the developments and technologies discussed in this book. Optical illusions come from the mind of the observer, but illusions are responsible for great beauty—they are what make art possible.

THE FUTURE OF OPTICS

In a sense, the future of optics is already here. Lasers that sculpt a person's cornea to improve vision or strands of glass that carry messages of light to all parts of the globe were the stuff of science fiction just a few decades ago. Today they are commonplace.

Yet optics is not finished. No one knows exactly what the future of optics has in store, but if it is anything like the last 100 years, the effects on society will be considerable.

One future trend in the science of light might be an increasing reliance on adaptive optics. This branch of optics refers to the ability of an instrument to adapt or compensate for fluctuations in the path of light due to changes in the medium. Mirages occur when the boundaries between warm and cold air refract or bend light, as discussed in chapter 17, and stars twinkle because of similar atmospheric distortions. The distortion created by the shifting atmosphere is a big problem for astronomers, who would like to have telescopes and other optical instruments that adjust themselves to the changing conditions, providing a clear view despite light's zigzag path through air.

One method of adaptive optics is the use of a "rubber" mirror. The mirror is not actually rubber but instead is made of some kind of deformable, reflective substance. Sensors measure light to establish the phases and other properties of the arriving waves based on a reference beam, which may be a bright star in the case of astronomical applications. Small motors change the shape of the mirror to compensate for distortions caused by the atmosphere so the light under study will remain focused and produce relatively clear images. In order to work properly, the adaptive mechanism has to be fast—to correct for atmospheric distortion, a mirror has to change shape several hundred times every second. The Keck Observatory in Hawaii already uses adaptive optics, but deformable mirrors are currently expensive and difficult to make, limiting their application today. In the future, however, optical devices of great precision may be more wiggly than rigid.

Advances in optics can affect many aspects of light beyond scientific research in astronomy. The U.S. government has recently felt the need to redesign $10 and $20 bills in the effort to foil counterfeiters; as photography and digital scanning improves, further changes in currency can be expected. This will raise the cost of printing money—and perhaps even force financial transactions to rely solely on credit or debit devices. But if money continues to circulate as paper bills, it will not be surprising if the designs become so elaborate and beautiful that people are reluctant to spend them (and not just for economic reasons).

Entertainment may also change. Movies are usually made with cameras to film real people—actors and actresses—playing the characters. Cartoons are drawn and presented with the aid of computers and computer graphics and obviously do not represent real scenery or individuals, no matter how well they are drawn. But the speed of computers is increasing, and as optical rendering of people, animals, and backgrounds becomes more realistic, cartoons approach a more lifelike quality. The animated film *Finding Nemo*, for example, showed stunning underwater scenes. Modern computer games are also visually impressive. In the future, the skill of computer programmers and the optics of perspective, art, and illusion may make cameras and live actors and actresses obsolete. Every movie will be a "cartoon," although it will be almost impossible to tell.

But perhaps the most significant impact of optics will arrive when, and if, people achieve a more complete understanding of light. The wave-particle duality of light is perplexing and, at least to some scientists, unsatisfying. There may not turn out to be a more satisfying explanation since nature does not have to conform to any rule that says it has to be comprehensible to the minds of humans. Yet science has risen to the occasion again and again in the past, solving mysteries of planetary motion, electricity, magnetism, and many others that seemed impossible to understand at first. Perhaps there is a better theory of light waiting to be found, and perhaps it will be found in the near future. Should this theory exist and explain something as perplexing as wave-particle duality, it will undoubtedly have powerful effects not only on science but on all of technology as well.

Photonics has not yet caught up with electronics, but the day may soon arrive when light can do all that electricity can—and more. There is great order in nature, and there is great order and beauty in optics. The power of light to illuminate is strong, and so much more is yet to come.

GLOSSARY

AC   Alternating current, a flow of electric charges that periodically changes direction.

accommodation   A change in the shape of the eye's lens in order to adjust the focus.

astigmatism   Irregularities in the cornea causing blurry vision.

blind spot   The exit of the optic nerve out the back of the eye creates an area of the retina without photoreceptors, so there is a blind spot in the field of view of the eye at this point.

CCD   Charge-coupled device, an array of electrical components that are sensitive to light.

CD   Compact disc, which stores music or computer data in a series of pits or bumps that are read by a laser.

cell   In biology, the basic unit of life, consisting of a membrane surrounding an aqueous solution of biological molecules and associated structures.

cerebral hemisphere   One of the two halves in which the brain is divided; the left and right hemispheres of the brain each consist of an outer covering of cells called the cerebral cortex and other groups of cells within.

chromatic aberration   The focusing defect caused by the tendency of a glass lens to refract different wavelengths (colors) of light to a different spot.

coherent   Acting together, as group of photons (or waves) of light that have a definite phase relationship and behave as a single unit.

concave lens   A lens that is thinner in the middle than the edges, causing light to diverge.

concave mirror   A mirror that curves inward, converging reflecting light.

converge   To move toward the same point.

convex lens   A lens that is thicker in the middle than the edges, causing light to converge.

convex mirror   A mirror that curves outward, diverging reflecting light.

cornea   The transparent part of the outer covering of the eye.

diffraction   A change in path of a light wave as it moves through an opening or around an obstacle.

dispersion   The spreading of light into its component frequencies.

diverge   To move away or apart.

DVD   A disc that codes video or computer data in a series of pits or bumps, read by a laser.

dye   A substance usually dissolved in water and used to color objects such as cloth.

electromagnetic radiation or wave   Energy consisting of propagating electric and magnetic fields.

electron   A negatively charged particle and component of an atom, where it orbits the positively charged nucleus.

field   A region of space where a force acts.

focal length   The distance from the lens to its focal point.

focal point   The point at which rays converge.

fovea   A small area in the retina, rich in cones, upon which falls light from the center of gaze.

frequency   The number of times an event occurs per unit time; for waves, the number of cycles per unit time (usually seconds).

gamma ray   Electromagnetic radiation of a frequency beyond 5×10^{19} hertz.

geometrical optics   The study of light rays and their paths through optical systems.

gigahertz   One billion hertz.

hertz   A unit of frequency, equal to the number of cycles per second.

HST   *Hubble Space Telescope*, launched by NASA in 1990 and repaired in 1993.

hyperopia   Farsightedness, the condition in which the eye tends to focus objects behind the retina, resulting in blurry vision for all except distant objects.

illusion, optical   A deceptive or misinterpreted image.

index of refraction   The speed of light in a vacuum divided by the speed of light through a particular material.

infrared   Invisible electromagnetic radiation with a frequency slightly lower than red light; the frequency range is roughly 300 billion hertz to 430 trillion hertz.

interface   A meeting of two materials; a boundary.

interference   A combination of waves, in which the resultant wave can be brighter or darker depending on the phase relationships of the combining waves.

interference fringes   Bright and dark bands resulting from interference.

interferometer   An instrument to measure distance or speed based on the interference of waves.

JWST   *James Webb Space Telescope*, a future NASA project.

laser   Light amplification by stimulated emission of radiation, producing brightly intense beams of coherent light.

law of reflection   A light ray reflecting from a surface makes the same angle with respect to the normal as the original (incident) ray.

law of refraction   An equation describing the refraction of light, relating θ_i, the angle the original ray makes (called the angle of incidence), θ_r, the angle of the refracted ray, n_i, the index of refraction for the material that the light leaves, and n_r, the index of refraction for the material it enters: $n_i \sin \theta_i = n_r \sin \theta_r$.

lens   A transparent, carefully shaped object that refracts light.

LISA   Laser Interferometer Space Antenna, a future NASA project to put a precision interferometer in space.

microwaves   Electromagnetic waves ranging from one to 300 gigahertz.

mirage   Refraction by the atmosphere that causes images of objects to be seen, sometimes in an inverted or magnified form, in places where the objects are not really located.

myopia   Nearsightedness, the condition in which the eye tends to focus objects in front of the retina, resulting in blurry vision for all except nearby objects.

NASA   National Aeronautics and Space Administration, the government agency responsible for space exploration and technology.

normal   An imaginary line perpendicular to the surface of an object.

objective lens   A lens or combination of lenses in an optical instrument that is closest to the object under study.

optical illusion   *See* ILLUSION, OPTICAL.

optic nerve   A bundle of nerve fibers that carries visual information from the eye to the brain.

paraboloid　Having a cross section of a parabola, such as a curve representing the mathematical function x^2.

perspective　In drawing, the representation on a flat surface of solid objects or objects in a distance in a manner that conveys an impression of depth.

phase　A specific point in time, such as a crest or trough, in the cycle of a wave.

photon　A particle of light.

photonics　Technology using light.

photoreceptor　A cell in the retina that responds to light.

pigment　Grains or small particles of a colored substance.

presbyopia　Farsightedness associated with age and the diminishing flexibility of the lens.

primary colors　A small number of colors that, when mixed, form all the other colors.

pupil　An opening in the eye through which light passes onto the retina.

radio waves　Electromagnetic waves with a frequency below one gigahertz (billion hertz).

real image　Forms behind a lens and can be projected on a surface.

refract　The bending of light as it passes from one material to another.

resolution　The ability to distinguish small objects.

retina　The thin set of cell layers at the back of the eye that process the image formed by the cornea and lens.

SAD　Seasonal affective disorder, a depressed mood that strikes people in the fall or winter.

SDI　Strategic Defense Initiative, proposed by President Reagan in 1983 to shield the United States from incoming missiles, in part by using orbiting lasers.

sonar　Sound navigation and ranging, the use of sound to map objects in the surrounding area.

spectroscopy　The analysis of light with respect to its component frequencies.

spectrum　The set of frequencies composing a wave.

speed of light　186,200 miles per hour (300,000 km/hr) in a vacuum.

spherical aberration　Distortion of an image due to improper curvature of the lens or mirror.

total internal reflection　Complete reflection of light as it strikes a material with a lower index of refraction at a shallow angle.

transparent   Allowing the passage of light.

ultraviolet   Invisible electromagnetic radiation with a frequency slightly beyond that of violet light; the frequency range is roughly 750 trillion hertz to 2.4×10^{16} hertz.

virtual image   Produced by diverging rays that appear to be coming from a point; this kind of image cannot be projected on a surface.

wavelength   The distance of one full cycle of a wave.

X-ray   Electromagnetic radiation of a frequency between about 2.4×10^{16} and 5×10^{19} hertz.

FURTHER READING AND WEB SITES

Books

Bloomfield, Louis A. *How Things Work: The Physics of Everyday Life*. 2nd ed. New York: Wiley, 2001. This exceptional college-level text explains the physics behind a wide variety of everyday phenomenon. Topics related to optics include fluorescent lamps, lasers, cameras, sunlight, and optical recording and communication.

Bova, Ben. *The Story of Light*. Naperville, Ill.: Sourcebooks, 2001. Written by a prominent author of science books and science fiction novels, this book covers all the technological and scientific aspects of the subject.

Clegg, Brian. *Light Years and Time Travel: An Exploration of Mankind's Enduring Fascination with Light*. New York: Wiley, 2001. A fascinating chronicle of the history of attempts to understand the nature of light.

Harbison, James P., and Robert E. Nahory. *Lasers: Harnessing the Atom's Light*. New York: Scientific American Library, 1998. A readable and enjoyable introduction to the world of lasers.

Hecht, Jeff. *Optics: Light for a New Age*. New York: Charles Scribner's Sons, 1987. Written by an author with a huge amount of experience on the subject, this book introduces young adults to the science and technology of light.

Hubel, David H. *Eye, Brain, and Vision*. New York: Scientific American Library, 1988. An excellent and accessible book on the physiology of the visual system, written by one of the most noted vision researchers of the 20th century.

Perkowitz, Sidney. *Empire of Light*. New York: Henry Holt, 1996. A wide-ranging account of the theories and experiments associated with electromagnetic radiation.

Taylor, Jim. *Everything You Ever Wanted to Know about DVD*. New York: McGraw-Hill, 2004. A detailed description of video discs.

Web Sites

Arecibo Observatory homepage. Available online. URL: http://www.naic.edu. Accessed on November 14, 2005. News and information on one of the most prominent radio observatories in the world.

Davidson, Michael W. "Molecular Expressions Science, Optics and You—Timeline—Pioneers in Optics." Florida State University. Available online. URL: http://www.microscopy.fsu.edu/optics/timeline/people/index.html. Accessed on November 14, 2005. Biographies of a large number of optical scientists from ancient times to the modern era.

Force, Incorporated. "Fiber Optics." Available online. URL: http://www.fiber-optics.info. Accessed on November 14, 2005. This Web site contains a wealth of information on the history, technology, and applications of fiber optics.

Gemini Observatory homepage. Available online. URL: http://www.gemini.edu. Accessed on November 14, 2005. News and information on two of the largest reflecting telescopes in the world.

How Stuff Works. "How Light Works." Available online. URL: http://science.howstuffworks.com/light.htm. Accessed on November 14, 2005. An excellent summary of the science of light.

Krystek, Lee. "Mirages in the Sky." Museum of Unnatural Mystery. Available online. URL: http://www.unmuseum.org/mirage.htm. Accessed on November 14, 2005. An illustrated description of the phenomenon of mirages.

Kulesa, Craig. "What is Spectroscopy?" Available online. URL: http://loke.as.arizona.edu/~ckulesa/camp/spectroscopy_intro.html. Accessed on November 14, 2005. An introduction to the science and equipment of spectroscopy.

Lucent Technologies. "What Is a Laser?" Available online. URL: http://www.bell-labs.com/history/laser/laser_def.html. Accessed on November 14, 2005. A basic description of lasers, from the Web site of Bell Labs. Bell Labs, now a part of Lucent Technologies, is a research laboratory that has been involved in many technological innovations, including lasers.

National Aeronautics and Space Administration. Imagine the Universe. "Electromagnetic Spectrum." Available online. URL: http://imagine.gsfc.nasa.gov/docs/introduction/emspectrum.html. Accessed on November 14, 2005. A richly illustrated introduction to the spectrum of electromagnetic radiation.

———. "James Webb Space Telescope." Available online. URL: http://www.jwst.nasa.gov. Accessed on November 14, 2005. Information on the development of the next-generation space telescope.

———. "Laser Interferometer Space Antenna (LISA)." Available online. URL: http://lisa.jpl.nasa.gov. Accessed on November 14, 2005. News and information on plans for an ambitious project to measure gravitational waves and other phenomena in space using a laser interferometer.

————. "Space Optics." Available online. URL: http://optics.nasa.gov. Accessed on November 14, 2005. Descriptions of the various optical projects and technologies at NASA.

National Ignition Facility homepage. Available online. URL: http://www.llnl. gov/nif. Accessed on November 14, 2005. News and information on the development of the world's largest laser, to be used for studies on fusion, energy, and astrophysics.

National Institute of Standards and Technology homepage. Available online. URL: http://www.nist.gov. Accessed on November 14, 2005. News and information about the government agency responsible for advancing measurement science and standards.

Sierra Vista Faculty. "Perspective." Available online. URL: http://www. sierravista.wuhsd.k12.ca.us/basicart/perspective.htm. Accessed on November 14, 2005. This Web page is one of a series of basic art lessons. This unit teaches beginning art students the fundamentals of perspective.

Space Telescope Science Institute. "Hubble Space Telescope." Available online. URL: http://hubblesite.org. Accessed on November 14, 2005. This site contains information on the *Hubble Space Telescope*, along with plenty of breathtaking images of galaxies, nebulae, planets, and other astronomical bodies.

Spittin' Image Software, Inc. "Optical Illusions." Available online. URL: http://www.colorcube.com/illusions/illusion.htm. Accessed on November 14, 2005. Illustrations of some of the most interesting optical illusions.

Very Large Array (VLA) homepage. Available online. URL: http://www.vla. nrao.edu. Accessed on November 14, 2005. News and information on the array of radio telescopes, located in New Mexico, which provide excellent resolution of radio sources in the sky.

Web Exhibits. "Colors: Why Things are Colored." Available online. URL: http://webexhibits.org/causesofcolor. Accessed on November 14, 2005. A thorough examination, with many examples, of the causes of color.

Wikipedia. "Light." Available online. URL: http://en.wikipedia.org/wiki/ Light. Accessed on November 14, 2005. This entry in Wikipedia, the Internet's free encyclopedia, gives a good overview of the experimental and theoretical aspects of the study of light.

INDEX